1973

the golden year of

PROGRESSIVE ROCK

Geoff

sonicbondpublishing.com

Sonicbond Publishing Limited
www.sonicbondpublishing.co.uk
Email: info@sonicbondpublishing.co.uk

First Published in the United Kingdom 2022
First Published in the United States 2022

British Library Cataloguing in Publication Data:
A Catalogue record for this book is available from the British Library

Copyright Geoffrey Feakes 2022

ISBN 978-1-78952-165-8

Typeset in ITC Garamond & ITC Avant Garde
Printed and bound in England

Graphic design and typesetting: Full Moon Media

1973
the golden year of
PROGRESSIVE ROCK

Geoffrey Feakes

SONICBOND

sonicbondpublishing.com

This book is dedicated to the memory of Christopher John Feakes (23 December 1943 – 9 October 2021). He was my brother, my inspiration and a true music fan.

Prologue

In 1973, spiralling inflation and an oil crisis in the Middle East resulted in economic turmoil on a global scale. America had its distractions with the end of the Vietnam Wara, the Watergate scandal and the opening of New York's World Trade Center. To combat inflation in Britain, the Conservative government introduced a wage freeze and in response, 1.6 million workers went on strike. To conserve fuel, the notorious 'three-day week' was introduced at the end of the year. More worryingly, the ongoing troubles in Northern Ireland spread to the streets of England with bombs in London and Manchester. In the Eastern Bloc countries, rock itself was under threat from the authorities, which they deemed subversive, forcing many bands underground.

On the sporting front, it being an odd – as opposed to an even – number year, there were no Olympics or World Cup, but in January, the Miami Dolphins won the American Super Bowl VII, Sunderland beat Leeds in the English FA Cup and, in July, Billie Jean King triumphed at Wimbledon. A trip to the cinema was also a welcome diversion and although multiplexes were in their infancy, there were plenty of choices. *American Graffiti* was a nostalgic homage to 1960s Americana, while *The Exorcist* was scaring the audience and introducing them to the delights of *Tubular Bells* at the same time. On the action front, Roger Moore was making his Bond debut in *Live and Let Die* aided by Paul McCartney's title song, while Bruce Lee achieved legendary status in *Enter the Dragon* before his untimely death on 20 July that year.

If you stayed at home in the UK, you had just three TV channels to choose from, but it did include *Monty Python's Flying Circus* and *The Old Grey Whistle Test*, essential viewing for those of a certain age and disposition. For the less discriminating viewer, the annual Eurovision Song Contest took place in Luxembourg, where typically the host country received the most votes. If reading was more your thing, Richard Bach's *Jonathan Livingston Seagull* was a best seller in 1973 and the film version, along with Neil Diamond's excellent soundtrack album, was released the same year. J. R. R. Tolkien's *The Lord of the Rings* was more popular than when it was first published in 1954.

Unlike FM radio in the USA, the daytime airwaves in the UK provided little in the way of credible entertainment, with bland MOR, glam-pop, and Osmond-mania dominating the singles chart. In the weekday evenings, Radio One DJs Bob Harris and John Peel played more palatable fare as did progressive rock enthusiast Alan Freeman on Saturday afternoons. For insomniacs, Kid Jensen's *Dimensions* show on Radio Luxembourg specialised in prog although reception in the UK was very much hit and miss. With the internet and social media several decades away, the UK rock music press, including *Melody Maker*, *NME* and *Sounds,* were vital sources of information for the dedicated music lover.

Given the political and economic turmoil, 1973 was a year that some may wish to forget, but not your author. I was in my late teens, enjoying a vibrant music scene in the company of like-minded friends. Over the course of the year, I purchased around 80 LPs and I was fortunate enough to see many of the bands live. The average ticket price in the UK was £1, which, allowing for inflation, works out at around £10 today. Compare this with Genesis' 2021-2022 *The Last Domino?* tour where tickets began at around £150 and spiralled significantly higher. Vinyl LPs cost somewhere between £2 and £3 but housed in the ubiquitous gatefold sleeve; they were desirable items that provided 40 minutes of escapism.

Progressive rock faced stiff competition in 1973 with landmark albums coming from every corner of popular music, including David Bowie's *Aladdin Sane*, Steely Dan's *Countdown To Ecstasy*, The Eagles' *Desperado*, Alice Cooper's *Billion Dollar Babies*, The Wailers' *Catch a Fire*, Marvin Gaye's *Let's Get It On*, The Rolling Stones' *Goats Head Soup*, The Allman Brothers Band's *Brothers and Sisters*, The Beach Boys' *Holland*, Paul Simon's *There Goes Rhymin' Simon*, Van Morrison's *Hard Nose the Highway* and Bruce Springsteen's debut *Greetings from Asbury Park, N.J.*

Prog rock held its own and bands like Yes, ELP, Jethro Tull and Pink Floyd enjoyed album and concert sales that rivalled populist acts like The Who and The Rolling Stones. It was that rare instance where unprecedented artistic credibility went hand in hand with commercial success, achieved with little in the way of radio or TV exposure.

The long-playing record had evolved from a collection of unrelated songs to a work of artistic expression. Although concept albums would become synonymous with progressive rock, seemingly everyone in 1973, from The Osmonds to The Carpenters to The Who had an ambitious song cycle up their sleeve. For the discerning music lover, it was possible to journey to the dark side of the moon, take a dip in topographic oceans and encounter pixies from a distant planet in a flying teapot and still be home in time for larks' tongues in aspic.

Geoffrey Feakes, October 31st 2021

1973: *the golden year of*
PROGRESSIVE ROCK

Contents

Introduction

Before delving into the music of 1973, let's wind the clock back a further three years to one lunchtime in early 1970. Here, you will find the author sitting in an empty classroom during my final year at school. Aware of my love of The Beach Boys, The Moody Blues, John Barry, Ennio Morricone, Dvořák and Sibelius, my music teacher played a record which she felt would appeal to my eclectic – some would say eccentric – tastes. It was unlike anything I had heard before and the final track blew my adolescent mind. I was entranced by the grandiose orchestral strings – which I later discovered to be a keyboard – vibrant rhythms and the male singer's untypically angelic tones. It was neither rock nor classical but somehow a fusion of both. The record in question was *In the Court of the Crimson King*, which not only defined my musical tastes over the next ten years, it arguably kick-started a genre.

It's worth noting that King Crimson's 1969 debut masterpiece was – with the exception of its successor *In the Wake of Poseidon* – unlike subsequent releases by them or any other band for that matter. It stands as a unique achievement, and that's true of progressive rock itself; a vast and diverse musical subject consisting of many styles that's almost impossible to categorise.

While 'progressive rock' is not, as I recall, a term that I or my friends commonly used in the early 1970s, it was certainly in use at the beginning of the decade, as evidenced by the *Bath Festival of Blues & Progressive Music* staged in June 1970. There was, however, a tendency to use it as a catch-all term for bands and musicians that played a variety of rock, whether it be heavy, folk, blues or symphonic. The UK music weekly *Melody Maker,* on the other hand, was still regularly applying the term 'pop' in 1970 to a wide variety of acts regardless of styles.

Everyone familiar with the genre will have an opinion on what defines a progressive rock record, but the chances are it will be different from the next person's interpretation. In an article I wrote in 2015, I posed the following as a possible definition. It's by no means definitive and perhaps a little too wordy, but here it is anyway:

It's a form of rock music, often structured in long, complex passages that's primarily not intended for dancing and therefore largely avoids the standard beat with timbre and texture more important. Performed by highly skilled musicians, it requires significantly more commitment by the listener to fully appreciate than is typical of most popular music.

Born out of pop-rock, jazz, folk, psychedelic, classical and blues, progressive rock is a hybrid that encompasses numerous strands that are as varied as the practitioners themselves. When prog is mentioned, symphonic rock usually springs to mind, as exemplified by bands like Yes and Genesis. There is, however, a multitude of subgenres, related styles and regional variations with bands from the UK, North America, South America, Italy, Germany, France,

11

Ireland, the Netherlands, Scandinavia, Japan, Russia and Australia bringing with them their own distinct take on the genre. As an example, in 1973, The Enid and Journey formed in London and San Francisco respectively and two bands more contrasting it would be hard to find. It's arguable that progressive rock is not, in fact, a genre at all but a collective term for a variety of related musical styles that strive to be more adventurous than the pop-rock mainstream.

Without wishing to dismiss the vast and excellent body of music that has been released from the late 1970s to the present day, the golden age of progressive rock is generally regarded to be 1969 to 1976. The most influential bands were active during this period and the most pivotal albums released. 1971 to 1974 was an especially creative period and any one of these years would have been a suitable subject for this book. In 1973, many of the bands that had formed in the late '60s were at their peak, while others were making impressive debuts. Prog rock's so-called 'Big Six' – Yes, Genesis, ELP, Jethro Tull, King Crimson and Pink Floyd – all released milestone albums in 1973, two of which would court controversy. In short, it was the year the genre truly came of age.

If you need further convincing, then hold this thought; over the 1973 Christmas holiday, Yes' *Tales from Topographic Oceans* and ELP's *Brain Salad Surgery* were the highest-selling albums in the UK. Prog was in its prime, and as a teenager with an insatiable musical appetite, I awaited each new album and concert with the anticipation of an expectant father.

Not everyone shared my enthusiasm, as certain factions of the music press demonstrated. Even the critics that had greeted prog rock with open arms were showing signs of discontent and when the backlash came, two of the biggest bands were on the receiving end. It was also a strange state of affairs in the UK where, despite huge album sales and sell-out concerts, even the more popular prog acts were little known to the general public whose exposure to popular music was limited to daytime radio and the weekly TV show *Top of the Pops*. Even in 1973, progressive rock was considered to be part of the counterculture.

To put 1973 into its musical perspective, this book is divided into two main parts, with the first providing a detailed overview of the year. This is broken down into subheadings, beginning with a brief history of prog prior to 1973. The subsequent sections discuss related aspects of the genre, including symphonic, the Canterbury scene, Krautrock, fusion, prog folk, art rock, space rock, hard rock, live work, critical reception and album artwork. Unless stated otherwise, all albums discussed will be 1973 releases, and – if known – the title will be followed by the month of release in the UK, e.g. *Genesis Live* (July).

Many of the bands and artists discussed will be familiar names, some unknown and some will surprise, but such was prog's widespread appeal in 1973, acts not normally associated with the genre displayed distinct progressive traits. Prog rock was popular – and believe it or not, fashionable – in the early 1970s and consciously or not, artists absorbed, recycled and fed back in a process of cross-pollination that blurred the musical boundaries. Although the term 'progressive rock' was not in common parlance at the time and the musical divides – if any – were not so obvious to consumers like myself, critics were quick to pigeonhole. Yes, Genesis and ELP, for example, were often collectively exalted – or dismissed – in a single sentence, despite their distinct musical styles.

The second part of the book examines in detail twenty key studio albums. If you have read any of the books in the *On Track* series from Sonicbond Publishing, then you will be familiar with the format. I should add that this is not intended as a 'Best of 1973' nor is it my twenty favourite albums of the year, even though many of those discussed I purchased in 1973 and remain in my vinyl collection to this day. Hopefully, it provides a broad representation of the rich and diverse prog-related releases that year, ranging from the melodic and symphonic to the complex and challenging with a good deal in between. The book concludes with an 'Epilogue' which provides an overview of post-1973 activities, including the influence of the early 1970s on subsequent and contemporary progressive rock.

As an avid rock fan in 1973, my experiences and recollections are no doubt reflected in the book. Almost inevitably, I will disappoint some by my omissions while others may question my inclusions. In truth, attempting to define what is a progressive rock band or indeed a progressive rock album is arbitrary, as is deciding if said band and their labour of love is good or bad. No opinion is final, and one person's masterpiece is likely to be someone else's overrated dirge. To quote the old saying, you can't please all of the people all of the time, and in my experience, progressive rock fans – like the music itself – can be very demanding. Long may it remain so.

Part One
In the Beginning

The original plan was for Peter Knight to do the real Dvořák stuff in between our rock Dvořák bits, and I just knew we'd be crap at that.
Justin Hayward discussing The Moody Blues' *Days of Future Passed* – *Rock Society* magazine, 2013.

The origin of progressive rock has long been a source of debate with The Beatles' 1967 masterwork *Sgt. Pepper's Lonely Hearts Club Band* regularly cited as the catalyst. Although its status as the first prog rock – or indeed a concept – album is debatable, there's no denying that The Beatles encouraged other artists to follow in their creative footsteps. The commercial success also gave record companies the confidence to support this unprecedented artistic freedom that would continue into the 1970s. Songs became more ambitious (breaking the accepted three-minute barrier), subject matter more diverse (beyond simplistic personal relationships), less formal patterns (verse-chorus-verse), richer textures, less rigid time signatures and more complex arrangements. This shift from formulaic pop-rock saw many bands and songwriters take the folk and blues rock routes – the latter spawning hard rock and heavy metal – while others experimented with psychedelic, jazz, avant-garde and classical music forms, often referred to as proto-prog.

The Moody Blues' ambitious concept *Days of Future Passed* followed *Sgt. Pepper* by less than six months and linked pop and psychedelic rock songs with sweeping orchestral interludes. Other UK groups like Pink Floyd, The Zombies, Traffic, Procol Harum, Tomorrow, The Gods, Clouds, Family, Soft Machine, The Incredible String Band and The Nice were also shaping the beginnings of progressive rock and, significantly, in 1968, albums outsold singles for the first time.

The late 1960s saw the advent of song cycles, including the Small Faces' *Ogden's' Nut Gone Flake*, Pretty Things' *S.F. Sorrow*, *The Kinks Are the Village Green Preservation Society* (all 1968) and The Who's *Tommy* (1969). While musically, these were more mainstream than prog, they – along with *Days of Future Passed* – paved the way for the concept albums that would become associated with the genre. Thematic LPs, however, are as old as the format itself. In the 1950s, popular singers such as Frank Sinatra released albums with a linking theme or mood and recordings of musicals such as *South Pacific* and *West Side Story* where the songs drive the narrative, were hugely popular in the 1950s and early 1960s.

Many bands at the forefront of prog rock in the 1970s released their debut albums in 1969 and 1970, including King Crimson, Yes, Van der Graaf Generator, Renaissance, Genesis, Emerson Lake & Palmer, Barclay James Harvest and Gentle Giant. Meanwhile, established acts like Jethro Tull and Pink Floyd adapted their blues and psychedelic styles to this burgeoning musical trend.

When it came to influences, many of these bands cast their net far and wide. In Yes' case, for example, it included The Nice, US rockers Vanilla Fudge and the vocal harmonies of Simon & Garfunkel and The 5th Dimension. Keith Emerson, on the other hand, had a penchant for jazz virtuosos Dizzy Gillespie and Oscar Peterson. Like many bands when starting out, Yes' repertoire included cover versions, although in their hands, these became extended, instrumentally dense workouts.

The established media were slow to recognise the shift in public tastes, and in 1970, album centred – as opposed to singles biased – rock was still commonly referred to as 'Underground'. Although mainstream radio and television all but ignored rock groups unless they had a hit single, the UK weekly music papers – *Melody Maker*, *NME*, *Sounds* – and *ZigZag* magazine championed the new breed of adventurous musicians. *The Old Grey Whistle Test* rock show (launched on BBC TV in 1971), late-night BBC radio and *Radio Luxembourg* were especially supportive and essential viewing and listening for prog fans.

As progressive rock developed, then so did the musicians themselves as instrumentation became more diverse. Along with rock music's familiar guitars, bass and drums, keyboardists expanded their scope with multiple instruments at their fingertips, including organ, piano, electric piano, synthesizers and the ubiquitous Mellotron. More traditional instruments also found a home in progressive rock. By the time Gentle Giant came to record their *Octopus* album in 1972, for example, their sonic palette included trumpet, saxophone, clavinet, harpsichord, violin, cello and xylophone; all played by the band members themselves.

Virtuoso musicianship, developing technology – especially keyboards, sound systems and recording facilities – and the desire to write longer-form songs all contributed to the prog rock explosion. Although some bands, such as Procol Harum, Barclay James Harvest and Yes, recorded with orchestras, it was possible to create a richer – often symphonic – soundscape without the need to engage additional musicians.

1971 and 72 saw a succession of groundbreaking releases, including the classic trio from Yes – *The Yes Album*, *Fragile* and *Close to the Edge* – the latter being perhaps the quintessential prog rock album. It was not without its rivals in 1972, which included Jethro Tull's *Thick as a Brick*, Genesis' *Foxtrot*, ELP's *Trilogy*, *Focus 3*, The Moody Blues' *Seventh Sojourn* and Wishbone Ash's *Argus* to name but a few. In just a few short years, progressive rock had already established an impressive legacy. Could 1973 maintain the momentum?

Symphony to Synths

Symphonic rock; it sounds like 'strawberry bricks', it doesn't make any real sense.
Jon Anderson, 1972.

The Yes frontman's scepticism is understandable. Artists do not like being pigeonholed and, as such, are wary of labels, however well-intended. Conventional wisdom has it that the terms 'symphonic' and 'progressive' are synonymous, although arguably, they are not interchangeable. If progressive rock is an all-encompassing genre, then symphonic is its most accessible strand and, unsurprisingly, in the early 1970s, the associated acts proved to be the most popular and enduring. By 1973, bands like Gentle Giant, Van der Graaf Generator, Focus, Gentle Giant, Barclay James Harvest, Curved Air and Wishbone Ash were already familiar to genre fans while others such as Camel and Greenslade were just starting out. In this chapter, while not exhaustive, we will examine the rich diversity of symphonic album releases and band activities in 1973.

Although concept albums became commonplace and tracks grew longer, songs were not extended simply to fill the space available on a vinyl LP. The songwriters and musicians developed material with a dynamic range that required more than the average three to five minutes to be emotionally effective. Typically, symphonic songs consist of multiple sections and intricate time signatures and while the emphasis is usually on melody, aggressive playing is common to emphasise light and shade. These long-form song structures often reveal classical influences, particularly the Baroque period of composers like Bach, the Romantic era of Sibelius and Ralph Vaughan Williams and the early 20th-century neoclassicism of Stravinsky and Bartok. Side long – if not album-length – pieces soon became the norm. It's a common myth, however, that the classical repertoire was regularly plundered in the 1970s. True, musicians like Keith Emerson covered classical pieces with ELP – as he had done with The Nice – and bands such as Renaissance occasionally incorporated uncredited classical themes into their songs, but this was the exception rather than the rule. Both ELP and Yes were pivotal in adopting the sonata form in their extended works from 1971 onwards.

1973 was a particularly prolific year for Yes, releasing an unprecedented five LP's worth of music. Although poorly recorded, the triple live opus *Yessongs* (May) showcased Yes in their prime and was a top ten hit in many countries, while the double studio offering *Tales from Topographic Oceans* (December) took Yes to the top of the UK chart. Genesis also released live and studio albums, although *Genesis Live* (July) and *Selling England by the Pound* (October) were more modest affairs – in volume at least. ELP would attempt to outdo Yes the following year with their live triple *Welcome Back, My Friends, to the Show That Never Ends – Ladies and Gentlemen,* but in the meantime, they settled for their fourth studio album, *Brain Salad Surgery* (November).

Wishbone Ash also pulled off the studio and live double punch in 1973 with *Wishbone Four* (May) and *Live Dates* (December). The former was a disappointment for many fans, while the latter includes songs from the pivotal *Argus* released the previous year, including a rousing version of the live favourite 'Blowin' Free'. Manfred Mann's Earth Band released *Messin'* (June) and *Solar Fire* (November), but just as significantly, they brought symphonic prog to the masses with their single 'Joybringer' based on 'Jupiter' from Holst's *Planets Suite*. On the subject of hit singles, when The Moody Blues' 'I'm Just a Singer (In a Rock and Roll Band)' was released in January, it climbed to number twelve on the Billboard chart and a reissue of the seminal 'Nights in White Satin' was more successful in 1973 in many regions including the UK and USA than it had been in 1967. Otherwise, the Moodies were inconspicuous album wise in 1973, as was Van der Graaf Generator, Barclay James Harvest, Supertramp and Jade Warrior.

VdGG folded the previous year, but lead singer and principal songwriter Peter Hammill kept the flame burning with his second solo album *Chameleon in the Shadow of the Night* (May). Musically, it maintains the spirit of VdGG and the band members are all present. They regrouped in 1975, but in the meantime, their excellent version of George Martin's 'Theme One' appeared on the Charisma Records sampler *One More Chance,* released in 1973. BJH were dropped by EMI's prog label Harvest Records due to poor record sales and spiralling costs – they often toured with an orchestra – so they were between labels in 1973. Jade Warrior were also without a record contract and temporarily disbanded while Supertramp spent a good deal of 1973 recruiting new members.

Yes keyboardist Rick Wakeman released his debut album *The Six Wives of Henry VIII* (January), while the band's refugees also had a busy year. *One Live Badger* featuring Wakeman's predecessor Tony Kaye was recorded during a show opening for Yes at London's Rainbow Theatre the previous year. It features some fine songs, including 'Wind of Change' sung by David Foster, who along with Jon Anderson, had been a member of 1960s pop group the Warriors. Badger released just one further album, the disappointing *White Lady* in 1974, before calling it a day. *Out of Our Hands* was the third and final album from Flash, the band formed by ex-Yes guitarist Peter Banks. Musically, Flash continued from where Yes' second album *Time and a Word* left off and were a fine showcase for Banks' underrated guitar talents. Unfortunately, the band folded following Banks' abrupt departure in the midst of an American tour. His debut solo album *Two Sides of Peter Banks* followed in 1973, a jam-fest with an impressive line-up of guests including Jan Akkerman, Steve Hackett, John Wetton and Phil Collins. To round off a prolific year, Jon Anderson, Steve Howe and Alan White guested on Johnny Harris' *All To Bring You Morning* album, an incongruous combination of lush strings and jazz-rock, although the near fifteen-minute title track featuring the Yes men has an undeniable grandeur.

Another ex-Yes man, drummer Bill Bruford was recruited by Robert Fripp for a revamped King Crimson, resulting in the album *Larks' Tongues in Aspic* (March). Fripp also collaborated with Brian Eno for *No Pussyfooting* (November), influenced by the minimalist style of composer Steve Reich. Meanwhile, ex-Crimson lyricist Pete Sinfield – who had been recently working with ELP and PFM – surprised everyone with the enigmatic *Still* album featuring a lead vocal from Greg Lake on the uplifting title song. Speaking of ELP, Keith Emerson was credited with Moog programming on *Bump 'n' Grind*, the fourth and final album from Jackson Heights, fronted by his ex-The Nice bandmate Lee Jackson. Later in 1973, Jackson formed Refugee – basically The Nice mark two – with drummer Brian Davison and Yes keyboardist in waiting, Patrick Moraz.

Jethro Tull's sixth studio album *A Passion Play* (July) was popular with the band's worldwide fan base, although it was shunned by critics, especially in Britain and America. For Gentle Giant's fifth album *In a Glass House* (September), it was almost the opposite reaction. It's regarded as one of their finest and, although they had a strong following in the USA, Canada and Italy, it failed to pique the interest of UK record buyers and was rejected outright by their American record company. They had an original sound with medieval folk and classical influences, although their choppy vocal and instrumental arrangements are not too removed from that of Jethro Tull.

Compared with folk, pop and mainstream rock in the 1970s, as well as the contemporary prog and symphonic metal scene, female-fronted prog bands were a rarity in 1973. The exceptions included the classically trained Annie Haslam, whose impressive five-octave vocal range featured on *Ashes Are Burning* (October), the fourth album by Renaissance. When Curved Air released their fourth album *Air Cut* (April), charismatic singer Sonja Kristina was the only remaining founding member, but it did feature the debut of seventeen-year-old violinist/keyboardist Eddie Jobson. *Air Cut* has its moments, but unlike the first three albums, it failed to chart in the UK and Jobson moved on to replace Brain Eno in Roxy Music. His Curved Air predecessor formed Darryl Way's Wolf and released two albums in 1973, *Canis Lupus* and *Saturation Point*. Both feature impressive instrumental interplay with Way's violin to the fore, alongside future Marillion drummer Ian Mosley. Curved Air disbanded in 1973 and reformed the following year with Way returning for a reunion tour. Although small in stature, American Jenny Haan of Babe Ruth had a fiery stage presence and a voice to match. Her English bandmates included talented guitarist – and later successful producer – Alan Shacklock, who gave the band their proggy edge, evident on the near ten-minute title track of the second album *Amar Caballero*.

While British prog bands were popular in America in 1973, especially in the northeastern States, homegrown acts were beginning to make waves of their own. Although they were not released until March the following year, both Kansas and Rush recorded their self-titled debut albums in 1973. The name Kansas had been around since 1970, but it was in early 1973 that the line-up combined the talents of Phil Ehart, Steve Walsh and Kerry Livgren. Rush were a hard-rocking power trio from Toronto, Canada as was evident on the first album. Their prog rock qualities would evolve on later releases following the arrival of the incomparable Neil Peart in 1974. Hailing from Virginia and influenced by Genesis and Gentle Giant, Happy The Man had formed the previous year and although they spent a good deal of 1973 in the studio, it would be another four years before their eponymous debut saw the light of day.

Chicago band Styx also formed in 1972, but they had a more productive year, releasing two albums in 1973. Like Rush, they favoured hard rock riffs, but *Styx II* (July) and *The Serpent Is Rising* (October) also established the band's progressive rock credentials. The latter, in particular, showcases their vocal and instrumental talents, closing with a version of Handel's 'Hallelujah Chorus', which may very well have influenced 'Bohemian Rhapsody'.

Todd Rundgren is another singer, songwriter and musician that had a busy year. In addition to releasing the genre-hopping solo album *A Wizard, a True Star* (March), he fulfilled his prog rock aspirations with the formation of Utopia. Although the *Todd Rundgren's Utopia* album wasn't released until 1974, the bombastic fifteen-minute opener 'Utopia' was recorded live during their 1973 – 1974 American tour. A less familiar name, songwriter, keyboardist Michael – brother of Suzi – Quatro was briefly promoted as America's answer to Rick Wakeman. His 1973 album *Look Deeply into the Mirror* was more glam rock than prog rock, but it had its moments, especially the Keith Emerson-inspired 'Prelude In Ab Crazy'.

Back in the UK, 1960s veterans, Procol Harum were still going strong and although *Grand Hotel* (March) didn't chart at home, it did respectable business in most other countries, especially America and mainland Europe. Critical reception was mixed, as is the blend of pop and prog although the title song, in particular with its soaring orchestrations and choir, has a stately grandeur. Unlike *Grand Hotel*, Argent's *In Deep* released the same month boasted a hit single in the shape of 'God Gave Rock and Roll to You'. It was also a finely honed balance between Russ Ballard's tuneful pop-rock sensibilities and ex-Zombies Rod Argent's piano and Hammond led excursions.

1973 was not without its low points and several bands that had been otherwise productive since the late 1960s unveiled some of their least inspired prog-light recordings. In no particular order, these include Atomic Rooster – *Nice 'n' Greasy* (September), Spooky Tooth – *Witness* (November), Gravy Train – *Second Birth*, Rare Bird – *Somebody's Watching* and Beggars Opera – *Get Your Dog Off Me!* The saving grace on the latter is an excellent, Moog driven version of Mason Williams' celebrated instrumental 'Classical Gas', which was also released as a single.

At the opposite end of the spectrum, several bands released very promising debuts in 1973. The eponymous *Camel* (February) introduced the considerable talents of Andrew Latimer, Peter Bardens, Doug Ferguson and Andy Ward, who would develop into one of the most respected and influential prog bands of their era. The memorable six-and-half-minute song 'Never Let Go' became a live favourite and signposted greater things to come on albums like *Music Inspired by The Snow Goose*. Released the same month, the self-titled debut

19

from Greenslade boasted two keyboardists and was followed by the equally impressive *Bedside Manners Are Extra* (November), unified by Roger Dean's excellent artwork. Taking their name from a King Crimson song, Cirkus hailed from the northeast of England and debuted *One,* although the album is best remembered for its rarity value and the fact that the belated follow up did not appear until 21 years later.

From Northern Ireland, Fruupp brought with them *Future Legends* (October), featuring orchestral arrangements with a distinct classical baroque influence and Beethoven references. There are also shades of Yes, King Crimson and Genesis and It was the first of four excellent albums over a period of fewer than eighteen months before their untimely demise in 1976. Although multi-national, the core members of the equally short-lived ensemble Esperanto were Belgian and *Esperanto Rock Orchestra* was the first of three albums that revealed a style and presentation, not unlike the Electric Light Orchestra. Carmen were an Anglo-American collective and their debut album *Fandangos in Space* is – as the title suggests – a genuine prog rock curio and they went down a storm live. From Wales, Sassafras was one of the hardest working – and rocking – bands on the gig circuit but their debut *Expecting Company* failed to capture the energy of their live performance.

For other bands, 1973 was their swansong year as far as studio albums were concerned. Fronted by the gravel-voiced Roger Chapman, Family – who had formed in 1966 – left us *It's Only a Movie* (September) before their final gig at Leicester Polytechnic – a regular Saturday night haunt for the author – the following month. Appropriately, the album's closing song is entitled 'Check Out', although it's no sad farewell, being a funky, upbeat rocker. The aptly titled *Voice* was the second of only two albums from Capability Brown, who disbanded the following year. Side two features the impressive 21-minute 'Circumstances', one of the great, unsung prog epics of the 1970s and boasts some of the finest vocal harmonies committed to vinyl.

Jonesy released two albums in 1973, *Growing* and *Keeping Up* but were unable to capitalise on their obvious talents and disbanded soon after. For King Crimson and Mellotron fans in particular, both albums are worthy of investigation. On the other side of the world, Australian prog band Spectrum called it a day in April 1973, and as a parting shot, they left the studio recording *Testimonial* (July) and double live album *Terminal Buzz* (December). Despite a number 1 hit single in 1971 – 'I'll Be Gone' – and the patronage of Harvest Records, they remained little known outside their home country. Australia, however, was a strong market for British and European prog rock in the 1970s and many of the albums discussed charted there.

The European Alliance

Double Dutch! Focus crash charts with two hit singles and two albums.
Melody Maker front-page headline, 10 February 1973.

On 1 January 1973, Britain, along with Ireland and Denmark, entered the European Economic Community. By then, however, popular music had already demonstrated the spirit of European harmony with progressive rock at the forefront of the cultural exchange.

Focus was undoubtedly one of the most successful continental exports in the early 1970s and 1973 was a particularly high profile year for the Dutch quartet. Following a legendary TV appearance on BBC2's *The Old Grey Whistle Test* the previous December, they released the infectious 'Sylvia' in January, which reached number four in the UK singles chart. A re-recording of the 1971 single 'Hocus Pocus' also breached the UK top 20 in January and climbed to number nine on the *Billboard* chart. The two previous studio albums *Focus II – Moving Waves* (October 1971) and *Focus 3* (November 1972), also charted higher in 1973 than they had done on their initial release. Although tracks were recorded in May – and eventually released on the *Ship of Memories* compilation in 1976 – a planned fourth studio album was abandoned and *At the Rainbow* (October) released instead. Recorded at London's Rainbow Theatre on 5 May 1973, it's a live 'best of' notable for the fluid guitar playing of maestro Jan Akkerman and Thijs van Leer's scat yodelling during a typically extended 'Hocus Pocus'. Akkerman's showpiece 'Tommy' was composed by fellow Dutch band Solution and featured on their 1972 album *Divergence*.

Not to be confused with Focus' drummer Pierre van der Linden – his second cousin – the late keyboardist Rick van der Linden had a fondness for fusing rock, jazz and classical music. In addition to his original compositions, the album *Trinity* by Dutch band Ekseption features interpretations of works by Bach, Beethoven and Rimsky-Korsakov. After being unceremoniously dismissed from Ekseption in late 1973, he formed the band Trace, who released three albums before disbanding in 1978, marking his return to Ekseption.

Two bands especially popular in the Netherlands were Kayak and Earth And Fire. Kayak's 1973 debut *See See the Sun* spawned two hit singles, while Earth and Fire's third studio outing *Atlantis* with its eye-catching cover art, features an ambitious sixteen-minute plus suite based on the mythical island. Although *Atlantis* is patchy in places, it's a must for those who just can't get enough of those Mellotron strings. Although they formed in The Hague, Supersister were closer to the Canterbury scene in style and their concept album *Iskander* – based on the exploits of Alexander the Great – was one of three releases in 1973, bookended by two compilations. It features French percussionist extraordinaire Pierre Moerlen and is very jazzy in style with intricate keyboards, saxophone, flute and bass exchanges.

Alquin, another Dutch band with a Canterbury vibe, released their second album *Mountain Queen* and on Friday, 24 August 1973, they were one of the opening acts at the UK's annual Reading Rock Festival. Both on and off stage, they had a forte for lengthy instrumental excursions, although vocals combine harmoniously with guitar, keys, sax, violin and flute.

Genesis headlined the UK's Reading Festival on the Sunday and, earlier the same day, French ensemble Ange impressed the Genesis faithful – including the author – with their rich, Mellotron-like Hammond chords and the eccentric theatrics of frontman Christian Décamps. Their second studio album *Le Cimetière des Arlequins* is rated as one of their best and features some finely tuned, melodic songs, including a memorable cover of Jacques Brel's 'Ces gens-là'. Inevitably, however, it pales in comparison with Décamps' live performance. Another French musician with a distinctive approach to music is Christian Vander, the brainchild behind Magma and the extraordinary world of Zeuhl, more of whom later.

When Italian bands Banco del Mutuo Soccorso, Le Orme and Premiata Forneria Marconi entered the 'Rock Progressivo Italiano' scene they brought with them their own classical sensibilities. Appropriate given that both opera and violin music originated in Italy in the 17th century. Banco's third album *Io Sono Nato Libero – I Was Born Free* in English – is one of their finest, benefiting from classically inspired dual keyboards and operatic vocals. The fifteen-minute plus 'Canto Nomade per un Prigioniero PoliticoIt' weaves symphonic textures with powerful arrangements and acoustic interludes with hints of ELP. Le Orme were often compared to the UK trio due to their keys, drums and bass/voice combination, although their concept masterpiece *Felona e Sorona* – a huge hit in Italy – is in a class of its own. PFM were perhaps the most readily accessible to a non-Italian audience, mixing virtuoso complexity and melody in equal measures and *Photos of Ghosts* (October) is one of the most symphonic statements the genre has to offer.

That same year, PFM's bassist Patrick Djivas performed on a very different sounding album, *Arbeit Macht Frei*. It was the debut release by the radical, multinational jazz fusion combo Area and the title – *Work sets you free* in English – was a comment on the Nazis' second-world war propaganda. From Rome, Il Rovescio Della Medaglia took the classical influence one step further by incorporating themes from Bach's *Well-tempered Clavier* on the album *Contaminazione* recorded with a full orchestra. An English language version – *Contamination* followed in 1975. Another notable classically influenced album is Museo Rosenbach's concept *Zarathustra* (April). It has that distinctive Italian sound, exemplified by the twenty-minute title piece with rich Hammond and Mellotron timbres to the fore. It was the band's only album of the 1970s before disbanding in 1974. Acqua Fragile released their self-titled debut album and supported several British prog acts when they toured Italy, including Gentle Giant in October 1973. Bernardo Lanzetti's husky singing – a cross between Peter Gabriel and Roger Chapman – dominates and when Acqua Fragile disbanded in 1975, he brought the same vocal style to PFM.

Finland's Tasavallan Presidentti, founded by guitarist Jukka Tolonen played the second day of the Reading Festival and entertained the crowd with a pleasing blend of prog and fusion. Although there was no album release from the band in 1973, both *Lambertland* (1972) and *Milky Way Moses* (1974) entered the top 20 in Finland. Also hailing from Scandinavia, multi-instrumentalist Bo Hansson's album *Magician's Hat* (September) was an English reissue of *Ur Trollkarlens Hatt* released in Sweden the previous year. It followed the similarly themed *Music Inspired by Lord of the Rings* from the previous year, which, given the popularity of Tolkien's work, reached 34 in the UK album chart. Hansson's success outside of Scandinavia was unprecedented at the time and, musically, he draws on a variety of instruments, especially keyboards, to create a colourful musical world – although it's a far cry from the grandiose film scores of Howard Shore.

In 1973, Swiss composer and keyboardist Patrick Moraz recorded film scores in his native Switzerland before travelling to England to join Refugee, a jumping-off point for Yes. The legendary Greek musician Vangelis is another composer/keyboardist with a Yes and film music association. Electronic drones from his 1973 soundtrack album *L'Apocalypse des Animaux* were played to the band's audience prior to Stravinsky's 'Firebird Suite' and their entry on stage during the *Relayer* tour. The same year, Vangelis released the album *Earth,* which was in a more progressive rock style.

Canterbury Tales

I think it's a rather artificial label, a journalistic thing.
Hugh Hopper – *Calyx* Canterbury music website.

Nestled in the southeast corner of England, Canterbury is a historical city popular with tourists thanks to its proximity to the port of Dover and the channel tunnel link with mainland Europe. London is just 50 miles away, the hub of the UK music business, but during the 1970s, Canterbury was a cottage industry unto itself. The term 'Canterbury scene' was coined by music journalists and referred to bands and artists with links to the town, regardless of how tenuous. It also suggested a particular musical aesthetic that was left of centre, slightly avant-garde with a penchant for quirky lyrics and Monty Python-esque humour. In reality, the bands were as diverse as prog itself; Caravan, for example, had a pastoral side to rival Genesis while Soft Machine in 1973 were full on jazz-rock.

The catalyst for the Canterbury scene was psychedelic rockers, The Wilde Flowers, who were active from 1964 to 1967. The list of musicians that passed through the band reads like a Canterbury who's who and would form the basis of Soft Machine and Caravan, the two most popular acts on the scene. If you can imagine a family tree linking all the Canterbury bands, the branches would eventually find their way back to the aptly named Wilde Flowers at its roots.

Caravan's most acclaimed album is the 1971 *In the Land of Grey and Pink* but the 1973 *For Girls Who Grow Plump in the Night* is probably their most accessible. Soft Machine's 1970 double LP *Third* is generally perceived to be their pinnacle, but in 1973 they released two albums, *Six* (April) and – yes, you've guessed it – *Seven* (October). *Six* was another double LP, this time combining a live performance with a studio recording and it was the last to feature bassist Hugh Hopper who departed following the recording. That same year, he released his little known solo debut album *1984* – eleven years before the fact – inspired by George Orwell's dystopian novel.

Another former member of Soft Machine, singer-songwriter Kevin Ayers is one of the foremost talents of the Canterbury scene, and in addition to his solo album *Bananamour* (May), he worked with Mike Oldfield and pioneering guitarist Steve Hillage amongst others. *Bananamour* boasts a stellar cast of Canterbury – and non-Canterbury musicians – and the brooding, eight-minute 'Decadence' is a perfect showcase for Ayers' deep and moody vocals. In June 1973, another ex-Soft Machine-ist, Robert Wyatt, was permanently paralysed following an accident during a birthday celebration for Gong co-founder Gilli Smyth. Although it ended his career as a drummer and he was wheelchair dependent, he maintained a successful solo career. Wyatt was especially dismissive of the 'Canterbury' label, partly because he was born in Bristol, nearly 200 miles away.

The Canterbury bands and its musicians had a tendency to cross-pollinate, not least keyboardist Dave Stewart, and in 1973 he joined Hatfield and the North following the recently fragmented Egg. Although it wasn't released until February 1974, in the latter part of 1973, the Hatfields recorded their eponymous debut, which is rightly regarded as one of the finest albums in the Canterbury canon. Another influential keyboardist – Soft Machine's Mike Ratledge – was responsible for one of the scene's signature sounds, courtesy of his fuzzed Hammond technique. On 30 November, he joined Mike Oldfield and several other Canterbury associates for the second only live outing of *Tubular Bells*, recorded for broadcast on BBC TV.

Like several Canterbury musos, the founding members of Henry Cow, Fred Frith and Tim Hodgkinson studied at Cambridge University. They were one of the most experimental UK bands of the early 70s, as evidenced on their debut *Legend* (September). A mostly instrumental album, the delightful harmonies and Frith's violin on the concluding song 'Nine Funerals of the Citizen King' provides a serene conclusion. Had the band been more popular, their cover artwork would have been a boost for the sock industry. Like Henry Cow, Gilgamesh had a penchant for jazz licks and although their first album did not appear until two years later, they were very active on the gig circuit in 1973.

Although many of its leading exponents disowned the 'Canterbury' tag – in much the same way that German bands took offence to the 'Krautrock' label – it has become synonymous with a relatively short-lived but fertile period of British progressive rock now long gone. The musicians involved were seemingly free spirits, wandering like troubadours from band to band where musical expression took precedence over commercial preoccupations, and some remain active to this day.

Path to the Dark Side

It was a bloody good package – the music, the concept and the cover all came together.
David Gilmour – *Prog Rock* magazine, 2007.

Released on 1 March 1973, *The Dark Side of the Moon* has been documented in so many books, magazines and online articles; it's almost impossible to be subjective about progressive rock's most famous recording. It's not only one of the best selling albums of 1973, but it's also one of the best selling of all time and it's a prog concept album. The latter assertion has been disputed over the years, possibly because the song subjects are wide-ranging, encompassing mortality, commercialism, war and mental meltdown.

To frame *TDSOTM* in its 1973 context, it was Pink Floyd's eighth studio album and the labour-intensive recording by its creators Roger Waters, David Gilmour, Richard Wright and Nick Mason stretched from June 1972 to January 1973. Self-produced, the time spent in the studio with engineer Alan Parsons paid off, resulting in the most sonically polished rock album up to that point. So much so, the production almost – but not quite – overshadows the material.

The band road-tested *TDSOTM* in its entirety in 1972, although my lasting memories of the performance at Leicester's De Montfort Hall on 10 February is the state of the art quadraphonic sound system and the band's extensive jamming. By the time it came to recording, the songs were radically reworked and benefited from the inclusion of new material as well as piano, saxophone and backing singers. Although studio inventiveness like cross channel panning and double-tracked vocals added an extra depth, songs like 'The Great Gig in the Sky', 'Money' and the double-punch finale of 'Brain Damage' and 'Eclipse' are memorable in their own right, with or without the sonic embellishments.

The only blight on an otherwise untarnished album is that up until 2005, session singer Clare Torry wasn't given her due compositional credit for the stunning improvised vocal on 'The Great Gig in the Sky'. Probably the jewel in the crown, however, is the sublime 'Us and Them', which, almost 50 years on, still has the power to send shivers down the spine. Thankfully, the band have never been tempted to record a *Dark Side of the Moon Two* or *Return from the Dark Side of the Moon*. What an ant-climax that would have been.

Germany Calling

What does 'kraut' mean? Is it something positive or negative?
Holger Czukay of Can – *Prog Rock* magazine, 2007.

First used by the British press in the 1970s, it's surprising that the term 'Krautrock' has survived, particularly in these more politically correct times. Similar to the Canterbury scene in the UK, it refers not only to a region – in this case, Germany – but also a certain musical aesthetic that provided an alternative to the progressive rock mainstream in the early 1970s. Krautrock – or 'Kosmische' music – is characterised by avant-garde forms, polyrhythms, unexpected tempos, unusual rhythms, repetition and free jazz stylings. Experimental composers and musicians like Karlheinz Stockhausen, John Cage and Miles Davis were prime influences.

Formed in Cologne in 1968, Can were pioneering experimentalists, and their fourth studio recording *Future Days* (August), is one of the movement's more accessible recordings – although 'accessible' is not a word I use lightly in this company. Another album considered a genre classic is the self-explanatory titled *Faust IV* (September), although Faust were even more extreme. Partly recorded at the Manor Studio in Oxfordshire, the track titles feature Anglo-German cultural references, including the hypnotic opening instrumental 'Krautrock' and the quirky 'The Sad Skinhead' that follows.

More minimalist but still rhythm-driven, *Neu! 2* is – as the title suggests – the second release by former Kraftwerk duo Neu!. All instrumental, the lengthy opening track 'Für Immer' demonstrates their ability to engage the listener, trading complexity for a linear, melodic momentum. Their albums were produced by the legendary Conny Plank, better known for his work with Kraftwerk. They were also a duo at this stage in their career and the third album *Ralf und Florian* (October) saw them embracing the electronic sounds that would become their forte. The International success of *Autobahn* was just one year away. Plank also co-produced the 1973 self-titled album by prolific psychedelic trio Guru Guru who released *Don't Call Us – We Call You* the same year. Formed in 1968, they are one of the most musically freeform and politically active of German bands and still perform to this day.

Berliners Ash Ra Tempel released no less than three albums in 1973, *Seven Up*, *Join Inn* and *Starring Rosi*. Fronted by guitarist Manuel Göttsching, they specialised in freeform, psychedelic rock and *Join Inn* also features electronic legend Klaus Schulze. His second solo album *Cyborg* (October), was a double LP consisting of four side-long spacey soundscapes. Schulze was also a founding member of Tangerine Dream, although he had long since departed by the time *Atem* (March) was released, which contains their familiar Mellotron and synth washes. Featuring the core trio of Edgar Froese, Peter Baumann and Christopher Franke, the side-long title track is one of their most popular works and foreshadows the landmark *Phaedra* which was recorded in November 1973. Popol Vuh were also specialists in new age, ambient excursions and *Seligpreisung* features lyrics adapted from the Gospel of Matthew set to keyboardist Florian Fricke's piano-led backdrop.

Not to be outdone by Ash Ra Tempel, Embryo also released three albums in 1973 – *Steig Aus*, *Rocksession* and *We Keep On*. They also found time to perform at the UK's annual Reading Festival in August, where they entertained the crowd with a lively combination of jazz fusion and world music utilising traditional instruments like sax, violin and flute. Kraan are another jazz-rock combo that was active throughout the 1970s and *Wintrup* was their second studio release.

Like Guru Guru, Amon Düül II had a socialist agenda and their LSD induced psychedelic offerings were influenced by early Pink Floyd. The title of their seventh studio album *Vive La Trance* gives some indication of where they were coming from musically, and 1973 also saw the release of the self-explanatory *Live in London* recorded the previous year. The album *Utopia*, recorded by producer Olaf Kübler the same year, features various members of the band. Birth Control were another band with a taste for psychedelic rock, although their fourth album, the suitably titled *Rebirth*, saw a significant change in personnel. Still active in various incarnations, Jane hail from Hanover and their second album *Here We Are* treads a fine line between hard rock, prog and psychedelia.

Teutonic progressive rock in 1973 was not all avant-garde eccentricity and sonic experimentation; several acts had a transcultural synergy with their symphonic UK counterparts. Formed in 1969 with a name derived from H.G. Wells' novel *The Time Machine*, Eloy combined symphonic with space rock to harmonious effect, revealing obvious Yes and Pink Floyd influences. Their second studio offering *Inside* is characterised by powerful guitar and organ workouts and they are still going strong to this day. Hailing from Hamburg, Novalis released their debut album *Banished Bridge* which showcased their rich vein of keyboard-based symphonic prog. With an eye on the UK and American market, it's their only album sung in English. Later albums performed in their native language would be better received. From Munich, Passport were noted for their distinctive cover artwork, which linked all their albums, including *Hand Made,* and they were also a fine ensemble of jazz fusioners.

Bells and Whistles

This is the British album that has been called a breakthrough in the field of rock.
Virgin Records promotional advert in America for *Tubular Bells* (1973).

Tubular Bells is one of those unexpected albums that comes out of the blue every now and then and leaves an indelible mark on popular music. The album's phenomenal sales success and its significance in expanding the fledgling Virgin empire have been acknowledged by Richard Branson. But had it not been for the faith the entrepreneur put in this seemingly uncommercial instrumental album by a shy and relatively unknown musician, it may have never seen the light of day. Mike Oldfield was no ordinary musician-composer. However, he was one of a new breed of multi-instrumentalists with a prestigious talent and vision. After hearing his demos, the prudent Branson gave the recording sessions at The Manor Studio, Oxfordshire, the green light. Under the watchful eyes of engineers and co-producers Tom Newman

27

and Simon Heyworth, Oldfield painstakingly pieced the album together, meticulously overdubbing the various instruments, mostly played by himself. When it was released on 25 May 1973, *Tubular Bells* took everyone by surprise, even prog-seasoned music lovers like your author. It was a modern masterpiece, a work of art that drew from rock and classical influences but still struck a chord with the general record-buying public. Although he was inspired by minimalist composers like Terry Riley, Oldfield's long-form structures that ebb and flow with rich melodies and pastoral orchestrations that build to crescendos are influenced by Jean Sibelius' Fifth Symphony. His musicianship regularly earned him a place in music polls in the 'miscellaneous instrument' category.

Ironically, despite its pastoral charms, *Tubular Bells* would become synonymous with the horror movie genre. Sales were boosted when an excerpt was used in the 1973 blockbuster *The Exorcist* and it influenced John Carpenter's piano-led score for his 1978 groundbreaking slasher flick *Halloween*. It may have also had some bearing on Italian horror maestro Dario Argento's decision to use prog band Goblin for his soundtracks from the mid-'70s onwards.

As an indication of *Tubular Bells'* popularity, when my wife and I first met in 1981, we had very different musical tastes and it was one of only three albums we had in common. The fact that Oldfield successfully repeated the formula with subsequent successors is a testimony to the enduring appeal of *Tubular Bells*.

Land of Fusion

With that level of technical skill, we were suddenly light years ahead of everybody because we were no longer three chords and a back beat.
Bill Bruford, 2015.

Bruford's comment on the 1970s progressive music scene was indicative of the like-minded attitude that prevailed amongst the virtuoso musicians at the time. This was particularly evident amongst the exponents of jazz fusion which flourished in 1973 and was much admired by the King Crimson drummer.

Since the 1920s, America has cultivated a rich heritage of jazz music, and by the early 1970s, it had infiltrated the rock mainstream. Bands were combining horns with guitars and keyboards to produce a jazz-rock hybrid as evidenced on Chicago's *Chicago VI* (June) and Blood, Sweat & Tears' *No Sweat* (August), while Earth, Wind & Fire took the jazz-funk route with *Head to the Sky* (May). The Chicago horn section also played on *Unlock the Gates*, the fourth and final album by Gypsy – not to be confused with funk outfit American Gypsy – one of America's unsung prog bands of the early 1970s.

A jazz staple, improvisation, along with lengthy instrumental workouts, became de rigueur during live performances by the jam band fraternity, headed by the Grateful Dead. The Allman Brothers Band were similarly inclined, and on record, 'Jessica', which they released as a single in December 1973, is one of the most infectious guitar instrumentals of all time.

Taking a more esoteric approach, an elite collective of jazz musicians combined free jazz and improvisation with more formal structures that included rock, classical, funk and world music. Pioneers in this field were Miles Davis, Herbie Hancock, Larry Coryell and drummer Tony Williams, whose group Lifetime had a revolving door policy. Yorkshire born guitarist John McLaughlin was an original member and, with his own group Mahavishnu Orchestra, he became one of the leading lights of jazz fusion, resulting in the stunning *Birds of Fire* (January) and the live recording *Between Nothingness & Eternity* (November). McLaughlin also joined forces with Carlos Santana for *Love Devotion Surrender* (July), while the latter's band Santana combined jazz-rock with their familiar Latin rhythms for *Welcome* (November).

Although fusion, like symphonic rock, straddles international boundaries, by 1973, America was a hotbed of talent. One of the leading exponents, Weather Report, led by keyboardist Josef Zawinul, recorded their third album *Sweetnighter* (April) in less than a week. The thirteen-minute opener 'Boogie Woogie Waltz' with its funky shuffle rhythm and inventive electric piano and sax exchanges live up to its intriguing title. Like the Mahavishnu Orchestra, Chick Corea's Return To Forever struck a chord with the prog audience, and the tour to promote *Hymn of the Seventh Galaxy* (October) included dates in the UK where I witnessed them on stage at Leicester University. The album's centrepiece 'Theme to the Mothership' is a showcase for their improvisational talents and keyboardist Corea's flair for memorable melodies.

Shortly after leaving the Mahavishnu Orchestra, drummer Billy Cobham released *Spectrum* (October), which was much admired by his peers, especially one Phil Collins. The ten-minute 'Stratus' is a stunning combination of precision and improvisation. Another influential musician, Return To Forever bassist Stanley Clarke released his own debut album, the aptly titled *Children of Forever,* which featured Corea and drummer Lenny White from his parent band. The mesmerising 'Bass Folk Song' demonstrates why in the 1970s, he was regularly lauded as the world's best electric bass player.

The pioneers of fusion remained active in 1973. Herbie Hancock released the groundbreaking *Head Hunters* (October), which opens with the near sixteen-minute 'Chameleon', rightly hailed as one of the defining works in the jazz-funk canon. Larry Coryell offered *The Real Great Escape* and although he also sings, the title track puts his guitar talents front and centre. No less than two live double albums *Black Beauty: Miles Davis at Fillmore West* and *In Concert* (May), showcase the famed jazz trumpeter and his band. Meanwhile, legendary experimentalist Frank Zappa and The Mothers Of Invention unleashed *Over-Nite Sensation* (September), which features the explosive talents of French violin export Jean-Luc Ponty. The funky 'I'm the Slime' – which was also released as a single – and the eclectic 'Montana' both feature Tina Turner on backing vocals.

Fusion was not exclusive to America in 1973. In addition to some of the previously discussed Krautrock and Canterbury bands, especially Soft Machine,

English keyboardist Brian Auger formed Oblivion Express and released *Closer To It,* although he relocated to Los Angeles to do so. Closer to home, Scots-born Ian Carr's ensemble Nucleus released two albums, *Labyrinth* and *Roots,* and the latter in particular features excellent trumpet and sax interplay between Carr and Brian Smith. The short-lived Tempest – under the leadership of drummer Jon Hiseman – released their eponymous album, the first of only two studio recordings. In addition to Hiseman's tasteful rhythms, it's notable for guitar, violin and compositional contributions from the extraordinarily gifted Allan Holdsworth, evident on the concluding 'Upon Tomorrow'. He is also present on a live performance by Tempest in June 1973 that was recorded by the BBC for radio and released on *Under the Blossom: The Anthology* in 2005.

A name synonymous with the early 1970s was Japanese percussionist Stomu Yamashta. His 1973 album *Freedom Is Frightening* encompasses fusion, world music and progressive elements and an extract was used in the 1976 sci-fi oddity *The Man Who Fell to Earth* starring David Bowie. The virtuoso playing of musicians like Yamashta, McLaughlin, Cobham and Clarke would influence British acts like Brand X, U.K. and Bruford, although they were still a few years down the line. Meanwhile, across the English Channel, French collective Magma took jazz-rock and avant-garde to new, unexplored heights with *Mekanïk Destruktïẁ Kommandöh* (December).

No discussion on jazz fusion would be complete without mentioning American composer/keyboardist Sun Ra who released no less than three albums in 1973, *Astro Black, Space Is the Place* and *Discipline 27.* His extraordinarily prolific output over four decades before his death in May 1993 is matched by its eclecticism.

Space Oddity

I rather like the idea of being in the underworld rather than the overworld. We are a traditional band, a traditional space rock band.
Dave Brock of Hawkwind – *Rock Society* magazine (2019)

Although we've touched upon space and psychedelic rock in the Canterbury and Krautrock sections, it's a subject that warrants further investigation. Pink Floyd's debut album *The Piper at the Gates of Dawn,* released in 1967, is credited with launching the genre with its studio experimentation, extended semi-improvised instrumental workouts, distorted glissando guitar, spacey effects and pulsating rhythms. By the early 1970s, they had been joined by a number of other bands in the musical space race.

Like many of the bands discussed, Hawkwind formed in 1969, and by 1973 they had established themselves as the undisputed masters of space rock. While the list of members and contributors over the years is endless, the line-up responsible for *Space Ritual* (May) is the definitive, with spoken contributions from sci-fi scribe Michael Moorcock. A double LP recorded live the previous year, it captures the sonic assault of their legendary stage performance and is their highest-charting album in the UK, reaching number nine. They released the single 'Urban Guerrilla' in July 1973, although the subject was ill-timed and was banned by the BBC. Formed in 1968, another London based ensemble UFO – like Hawkwind – combined hard rock with cosmic overtones, although 1973 was a transitional period with the arrival of ex-Scorpions guitarist Michael Schenker in June.

Across the border, Welsh rockers Man were one of the most prolific bands of the 1970s and *Back into the Future* (September) was their eighth album since their formation five years earlier. A double LP, it showcased the band in the studio and recorded live at London's Roundhouse theatre in June. The album title pre-empts the movie *Back to the Future* by twelve years and is clearly a nod to The Moody Blues' *Days of Future Passed*. The same can be said for *Remember the Future* (November), the second of two albums released by Nektar in 1973 and a genre-defining classic. The previous recording ...*Sounds Like This* (June), is a lengthy jam-fest spread over four sides of vinyl, designed to capture the band's live sound.

While musical diversity was not uncommon amongst these bands, aspects they often shared with Pink Floyd was presentation and conceptual narrative. Theatrical stage shows with psychedelic lights and back projection were de rigueur, as was album titles and abstract lyrics ripe with fantasy and sci-fi imagery common to bands like Hawkwind, Nektar and Gong.

A band that ploughed their own, uncompromising furrow both musically and professionally was acid rockers The Pink Fairies. Their third album, *Kings of Oblivion* (June), had a troubled birth but was critically well-received. Led by Arthur Brown, who had a flair for theatrics, Kingdom Come's criminally ignored *Journey* (April) was their third and final album and a must for space junkies with its pioneering electronic effects. It was also the first to utilise a drum machine, although we won't hold that against it! Tracks like the three-part centrepiece 'Superficial Roadblocks' are a mind-blowing kaleidoscope of sounds, including prominent Mellotron choir and epic storytelling.

Formed by another charismatic frontman Daevid Allen, Gong are psychedelic space rockers extraordinaire. Although Allen hailed from Australia and Gong had an Anglo-French revolving door line-up, they had links to the Canterbury scene. Gong released two albums in 1973, *Flying Teapot* (May) and the equally eccentric *Angels Egg* (December), the first two parts of the so-called *Radio Gnome Invisible* trilogy, which remains their most acclaimed work.

To illustrate that space rock is not solely an all British preoccupation, we'll close this section with Hungarian pioneers Omega. Formed in 1962 and still active to this day, they are one of the longest surviving bands in the book. Although their unprecedented popularity was mostly restricted to their homeland, the eponymous *Omega* was one of several albums they recorded in English. The album *Omega 5* was released the same year in Hungary.

31

They regularly toured Eastern Europe – where at one time their music was considered subversive – but their commercial appeal never transferred to the west. Formed in 1971, Locomotiv GT were an offshoot of Omega and dabbled in prog and hard rock and they were also victims of government suppression. The 1973 album *Bummm!* was banned when guitarist Tamás Barta illegally defected to America.

Pretentious, Moi?

Progressive rock, a '70s musical landscape dominated by concept albums about dungeons and dragons, aliens and geese featuring hour-long song cycles with week-long instrumental solos – well, it felt like it.
Mark Radcliffe – *Top Ten Prog Rock* TV Documentary, 2001

There's a saying that people are often frightened of what they don't understand, but more often than not, they mock what they don't understand. To be fair to Mark Radcliffe, he's one of the more enlightened presenters and I suspect that when he made the above comment, he had his tongue firmly in his cheek. It does, however, reflect the media's general attitude towards progressive rock, which, in the documentary and many others, is presented as a musical dinosaur to be ridiculed. It's also typical of the ignorance surrounding the genre where, despite Radcliffe's assertions, concept albums are in the minority and you will hear longer solos on a jazz or blues rock album.

In 1973, progressive rock had its share of supporters and detractors in the media. The UK music press were mostly in favour, especially *Melody Maker* and journalists like Chris Welch, who championed bands like Yes, Jethro Tull and Genesis. *NME* writers took what was perceived to be a more hip attitude and were often scathing, while *Sounds* was generally in the favourable camp. In America, *Rolling Stone* magazine had a bias towards homegrown acts playing traditional rock and were generally wary of British prog bands. *Circus* magazine, on the other hand, welcomed prog and most anything else from across the Atlantic.

On BBC radio, daytime presenters were hamstrung by the rigid playlist system, but in the evenings and weekends, the records played often reflected personal tastes. Alan 'Fluff' Freeman's Saturday afternoon show reflected his prog preferences – he was a big ELP fan and occasionally introduced them on stage. The influential John Peel gave many of the bands discussed in this book major breaks in their early years when they performed on his legendary radio sessions. He was, however, more cynical when they achieved fame and fortune, typified by his infamous tirade against ELP after their debut at the 1970 Isle Of Wight Festival, which he criticised as 'A waste of talent and electricity'. Ironically, he and Keith Emerson became firm friends when they discovered they had a mutual passion for football.

Although on British television progressive rock did not receive the same coverage and respect afforded to other 'marginal' genres like classical, jazz and folk, bands and artists did occasionally appear in live performances recorded by the BBC. First broadcast on BBC2 in 1971, the weekly series *The Old Grey Whistle Test* was a major breakthrough. It showcased the bands and the music in a magazine-style format that included studio performances, album tracks and interviews, presented by the inimitable Bob Harris.

Over the years, books on the subject have often presented prog rock as elitist, typically favoured only by males from an upper-class background. Clearly, these writers were not part of the audience in 1973. Although a much-maligned and misunderstood genre, regularly criticised as being pretentious and self-indulgent, prog endures, thanks to a loyal audience that appreciates the music in all its weird and wonderful manifestations.

There's nowt so queer as Folk

Schubert didn't make it, but Fairport have just completed their ninth. Island Records promotion for Fairport Convention's *Nine* album released in October 1973.

When Bob Dylan toured the UK in 1966 and riled folk traditionalists by playing electric guitar, it marked a turning point. The wind of change in the late 1960s and early 1970s saw many acts on both sides of the Atlantic remove folk's preconceived barriers, although there had always been more to the genre than finger in the ear harmonies and lively jigs. The leading exponents were prepared to experiment, augmenting traditional instruments like acoustic guitars and fiddles with contemporary rock instrumentation. Despite often complex arrangements and virtuoso playing, songs with the emphasis on storytelling remained. Not surprisingly, the more esoteric elements of folk rock struck a chord with prog fans.

The term progressive folk would be coined much later – categorisation and musical boundaries were of little interest to the discerning rock fan in 1973. Assuming your record collection was organised alphabetically, then it's quite possible that Fairport Convention would have sat comfortably between ELP and Free. Despite there being an element of rivalry between bands – usually fuelled by the media – there was a sense of camaraderie as a result of shared tours, festivals, recording studios and record labels. Geordie folk-rockers Lindisfarne for example, toured with Van der Graaf Generator and Genesis in 1971 on Charisma Records' infamous 'Six bob tour' and the band's principal songwriter Alan Hull was an admirer of Yes.

Fairport Convention are one of the true innovators of UK folk rock and also one of the most prolific, releasing two albums in 1973, *Rosie* (February) and *Nine* (October). Fronted by singer/bassist Dave Pegg and fiddle player Dave Swarbrick, they were an accomplished quintet and *Rosie* also featured the talents of guests Ralph McTell and ex-members Richard Thompson and Sandy Denny. With her solo career in the doldrums, Sandy rejoined the band the following January. Formed in 1972 by the highly respected singer/guitarist Christy Moore, Irish folk quartet Planxty also released two albums, the self-titled debut and *The Well Below the Valley*.

Rick Wakeman's pre-Yes band Strawbs – fronted by Dave Cousins – all but abandoned their folk roots in 1973 with the release of *Bursting at the Seams* (January), which fully embraced prog rock. It includes the UK hit single 'Lay Down', which – like Focus' 'Sylvia' – was a jukebox favourite in student-friendly bars in 1973 and a rare instance of a hit single featuring a Mellotron choir. The album's other UK hit, 'Part of the Union', is a novelty sing-along that you either embraced or endured and climbed to number two in the UK chart.

A folk-rock singer-songwriter of some repute, Roy Harper, was on friendly terms with Jethro Tull, Led Zeppelin and Pink Floyd, which resulted in occasional collaborations. His sixth album *Lifemask* (February), includes the 23 minute 'The Lord's Prayer', which features contributions from Jimmy Page and ex-The Nice drummer Brian Davison. Another singer/songwriter/guitarist much admired by his peers is John Martyn. *Solid Air* (February) showcased his extraordinary guitar technique, which encompasses folk and jazz. Led by Scottish singer/songwriter Mike Heron, The Incredible String Band also took folk into non-traditional territories as is evident on their penultimate release, *No Ruinous Feud* (March). Hailing from Glasgow, String Driven Thing toured in support of fellow Charisma label band Genesis to promote the album *The Machine That Cried*. Also from Scotland, Al Stewart effortlessly combined folk and soft rock as exemplified on *Past, Present and Future* (October), which boasted the cream of UK rock and folk musicians.

Steeleye Span were probably the UK's most popular folk group in 1973 thanks to an a cappella version of the Christmas carol 'Gaudete' reaching number 14 in the singles chart in December. *Parcel of Rogues* (April) is one of their most successful albums with an iconic cover design. Donovan had several hit singles of his own in the 1960s and *Cosmic Wheels* (March) and *Essence to Essence* (December) marked a return to popular form. In 1977, he was a 'special guest' on Yes' *Going for the One* tour. On the other side of the Atlantic, another singer/songwriter with a strong 1960s pedigree, Tim Buckley, released his penultimate album *Sefronia* (May) before his untimely death two years later. A seminal folk-rock band of the late 1960s / early 1970s, Pentangle – boasting the influential guitar partnership of Bert Jansch and John Renbourn – split in 1973, leaving behind the compilation *Pentangling*.

On a more positive note, several bands released promising debuts in 1973, including Decameron with the aptly titled *Say Hello to the Band*, which skilfully embellished folk with prog. Gryphon's eponymous debut *Gryphon* (June) revealed their medieval influences, although their prog rock credentials were not fully realised until the 1974 albums *Midnight Mushrumps* and *Red Queen to Gryphon Three*. Another artist yet to find his prog folk feet is acoustic guitar virtuoso Gordon Giltrap. The album *Giltrap* has its moments, but it would be the following trio of *Visionary, Perilous Journey* and *Fear of the Dark* that would mark his classic period.

Like Gryphon, Amazing Blondel also favoured Renaissance and Baroque period instruments, including the crumhorn, recorder and harpsichord as evidenced on their fifth album *Blondel*. American prog folkies McKendree Spring preferred more contemporary instruments, including electric violin, Moog and Mellotron, which were put to effective use on probably their best offering *Spring Suite* featuring Roger Dean's unmistakable artwork. Another of Dean's paintings also graced the cover of *Lord of the Ages* by English trio Magna Carta. The ten-minute title song is arguably their finest. As 1973 was drawing to a close, Irish folk-rockers Horslips released one of the year's most powerful offerings, *The Táin*. A concept album, it refused to be pigeonholed with an uncompromising blend of Celtic rock, hard rock and prog.

He Ain't Heavy, He's My Brother

We were called a heavy rock band, and we quite liked that because we were very intense about what we did.
Ken Hensley of Uriah Heep (May 1985).

As discussed earlier, rock fans, for the most part in the early 1970s, cared little about labels and judged each band or artist on their own merits, regardless of styles. Rick Wakeman once observed that there are only two types of music, good and bad, and although he borrowed the line from Louis Armstrong – or was it Duke Ellington – and it is perhaps an oversimplification, it's not difficult to see where he was coming from. As a Genesis fan, for example, I was also a Deep Purple enthusiast, even though the ornate pastoral whimsy of the former is a far cry from the raunchy posturing and testosterone-driven lyrics of the latter. It would be a decade or more before bands like Dream Theater and Queensrÿche successfully combined complexity with heavy riffs, giving birth to the popular sub-genre progressive metal. Appearances can be deceptive, however; on closer examination, the similarities between hard and progressive rock in the 1970s become apparent. They are both performed by skilled musicians and often feature extended songs with dynamic shifts between light and shade and a conceptual narrative with a penchant for fantasy themes.

Like The Nice and Yes, Deep Purple were influenced by bombastic American rockers Vanilla Fudge, evident in Jon Lord's aggressive Hammond playing. Purple had a flair for high octane songs, as demonstrated on the iconic double live album *Made in Japan* and although it was released in December the previous year, it breached the top ten in North America and many European countries in 1973. It's arguably the band's finest hour – or 77 minutes to be more precise – leaving the studio offering *Who Do We Think We Are* (January) in the shade. The perennial 'Smoke on the Water' from the previous album *Machine Head* was also released as a single in May 1973.

Black Sabbath was Purple's main rival on the heavy metal scene and their fifth album *Sabbath Bloody Sabbath* (December) was their proggiest offering yet. It features friend of the band Rick Wakeman on piano and Minimoog. When Yes supported Sabbath the previous year on their tour of the USA, drummer Bill Ward was so impressed he remained a lifelong fan, enthusing, 'If you're a student of music, then go listen to Yes'.

Although Led Zeppelin started out as a blues-rock band, by 1973, they were one of rock's most versatile units. The album *Houses of the Holy* (March) encompasses various styles, although the prog rock excursions are thankfully more successful than their reggae pastiche. Bassist John Paul Jones laced the brooding 'No Quarter' with atmospheric synth embellishments and sweetened the balladic 'The Rain Song' with Mellotron strings. Both songs clock in around the seven-minute mark.

A band that ploughed their own furrow with a foot in both the hard rock and prog rock camps is Uriah Heep. This was a heinous crime as far as critics were concerned, but, despite the bad press and the usual internal disputes, a loyal fan base ensured the band endured. Their sixth album *Sweet Freedom* (September), was especially successful Stateside and the double LP *Uriah Heep Live* (May) was a chart hit around the world. Not unlike Jon Lord's role in Deep Purple, the Hammond playing of Ken Hensley was an integral part of Uriah Heep's ear-friendly union of heavy metal, prog and anthemic rock. He was also the band's principal songwriter and his debut solo album *Proud Words on a Dusty Shelf* was another 1973 success.

Art for Art's Sake

> I wanted to explore different styles of music. I didn't want any imitations and it kind of ended up being a collage effect.
> Bryan Ferry discussing Roxy Music on *CBS This Morning* (March 2019).

In the UK, the top ten best selling singles of 1973 included easy listening and novelty acts Tony Orlando and Dawn, Peters & Lee, Simon Park Orchestra, Gary Glitter, Jimmy Osmond and Perry Como. In America, Billboard's equivalent chart painted a more credible picture featuring soul artists like Roberta Flack and Marvin Gaye and singer-songwriters Jim Croce and Carly Simon. But this wasn't the full story; a slick, modern and ambitious vein of pop-rock was also gracing the charts and airwaves that year with progressive tendencies springing up in the most unexpected of quarters. Art rock, progressive pop, crossover prog – call it what you will, such terms would eventually be coined to label the music and artists discussed in this section.

Although pigeon-holed as glam rock, Roxy Music, like David Bowie, were more high art and one of the classiest acts of 1973, both visually and musically. They were rewarded with two top ten singles and their prog credentials are evident on the haunting 'The Pride and the Pain', the B side of 'Pyjamarama'. They also released two albums, *For Your Pleasure* (March) – Brian Eno's swansong – and *Stranded* (November). In April, they made a memorable appearance on BBC TV's *The Old Grey Whistle Test* performing the extraordinary 'In Every Dream Home a Heartache'. Like Roxy Music, the Electric Light Orchestra released two hit singles and two albums, *ELO 2* (January) and *On the Third Day* (November). The latter saw a shift from the classical style of the first two albums to a more prog-pop orientated sound, although the strings and Beatles influences remained.

Both Queen and 10cc released equally impressive self-titled debut albums in July. Queen's formula combined the hard rock of Led Zeppelin with the symphonic grace of Yes, while the multi-talented 10cc produced grandiose pastiches of 1950s / 1960s Americana as exemplified on their chart-topping 'Rubber Bullets'. Both bands benefited from stunning harmony vocals; in 10cc's case, it was the American west-coast style of The Beach Boys while Queen – and Freddie Mercury in particular – favoured European operetta influences. The *Queen* album sleeve featured the disclaimer 'and nobody played synthesiser' while Moog and Mellotron regularly featured in 10cc's songs.

Elton John is another artist able to balance well-crafted singles with ambitious album tracks. His second of two albums in 1973, *Goodbye Yellow Brick Road* (October), boasted the opening instrumental 'Funeral for a Friend', which, coupled with 'Love Lies Bleeding', provided a dramatic eleven-minute overture. David Hentschel was responsible for the stately ARP synthesiser arrangement and he would later produce Genesis' albums. Another album released the same month, The Who's *Quadrophenia,* also featured the ARP, which Pete Townshend skilfully harnessed to provide symphonic embellishments for his epic tale of a teenage Mod in meltdown. The title track and 'The Rock' are proggy instrumentals, while 'Love, Reign o'er Me' is a tour de force finale.

Other examples of populist, crossover acts to catch the progressive bug in 1973 came from the world of pop, hard rock, folk rock, even soul. During the late 1960s / early 1970s, Traffic were at the vanguard of pop-rock, experimenting with various styles, including prog. *Shoot Out at the Fantasy Factory* (February) features as its centrepiece the near fourteen-minute 'Roll Right Stones'. Similarly ambitious, Cat Stevens' *Foreigner* (July) devoted the whole of side one to the eighteen-minute plus 'Foreigner Suite'. The upbeat melody in the closing section is similar to Coldplay's 'Viva la Vida' released 35 years later. Stevens was an admirer of Stevie Wonder whose stunning *Innervisions* (August) took funk and soul to new artistic heights. 'Living for the City' is an epic piece of storytelling and although the single release is half the length of the album version, it doesn't diminish the song's potency.

To round off the year, Paul McCartney and Wings released *Band on the Run*, a winning combination of tuneful songs and impeccable arrangements, not least the orchestrated title song. It topped the charts in many countries, but it wasn't the only album from an ex-Beatle that year. They may have separated three

37

years earlier, but individually it was a prolific period, with George Harrison's *Living in the Material World* (October), Ringo Starr's *Ringo* (November) and John Lennon's *Mind Games* (November) bookended by Paul McCartney and Wings' *Red Rose Speedway* (April) and *Band on the Run* (December). The ex-members of the most influential group of the 1960s could still hold their own with the progressive vanguard of 1973.

The Show that Never Ends

A breathtaking melange of science fiction and fairy tale overlaid with a mystic dimension.
Review of Genesis' concert at The Roxy, Los Angeles on 17 December 1973 by Richard Cromelin – *Los Angeles Times*.

The vast majority of acts active in the 1970s released on average one studio album per year. It was the norm; record companies decreed it, fans expected it and the artist or band duly delivered. The recording sessions were usually followed by a lengthy promotional tour before a return to the studio for the next album. It was a constant cycle, an endless treadmill of recording and touring, which often took its toll on individuals and band morale. The Moody Blues were one such casualty and following a relentless world tour in 1973, they decided to take a hiatus and would not release another album until 1978.

Despite 1973 being a very productive year in terms of recording and album releases, bands still found time for extended touring. Although stage lighting, sound systems and equipment had improved, stage presentation at the beginning of the 1970s differed hardly from that of the late-1960s. With the exception of a modest lighting rig and a few effects, the only visual stimulant was seeing a favourite band in the flesh with a stack of Marshall amps as a backdrop. As the bands began to play larger venues and becoming ever more distant from the audience, changes were in the air and 1973 proved to be a pivotal year.

As albums became more ambitious, prog bands, in particular, pioneered equally ambitious stage shows that would set a template for the stadium rock of the 1980s and beyond. Individual band members like Ian Anderson of Jethro Tull also had a penchant for theatrics and when Peter Gabriel first walked on stage wearing a red dress, he surprised not only the audience but his Genesis bandmates as well. During the *Selling England by the Pound* tour, he wore face paint and a variety of costumes to characterise multi-part songs like *Supper's Ready* and *The Battle of Epping Forest*. When Genesis performed at the Reading Rock Festival in the UK on 26 August 1973, during the opening of *Watcher of the Skies*, Gabriel descended from the heavens on what to your author appeared to be a pyramid-shaped spacecraft. Earlier the same day, the enigmatic Christian Décamps of French proggers Ange captivated the 25,000 strong crowd with a far more modest prop – two hand puppets!

Another band with a penchant for theatrics was The Sensational Alex Harvey Band, who appeared at Reading the previous day and virtually stole the show. Harvey was a natural showman and from the album *Next...* (November), they performed the extraordinary title song and the hypnotic seven-minute 'The Faith Healer'.

1973 was a breakthrough year in America for many UK acts, including Genesis. In December, during a three-night residency at the Roxy Theatre in Los Angeles, one over-enthusiastic critic described them as 'The most significant rock band to happen since the Beatles'. John Lennon himself gave their profile a further boost when he singled out *Selling England by the Pound* for praise during an interview on American radio.

While coliseums and arenas in North America were the norm in 1973, in the UK, it was still possible to see prog heavyweights like Yes, Pink Floyd and Genesis in provincial theatres such as Leicester's De Montfort Hall, where *Genesis Live* was partly recorded in February with your author once again in attendance. Unsurprisingly, these were often instant sellouts and inevitably, in these pre-internet times, lengthy queuing was required to secure a prime seat. In the winter of 1973, I spent all night in freezing conditions outside London's Royal Festival Hall on the banks of the River Thames. My reward was second-row tickets for Rick Wakeman's debut performance and recording of *Journey to the Centre of the Earth* the following January. On the night of the concert, I was sitting directly behind Steve Howe and Chris Squire, although curiously, I don't recall seeing either of them in the queue two months earlier!

In 1973, Yes' stage set underwent a dramatic overhaul. Until April, they were still touring *Close to the Edge* and the visual highlight was a revolving mirror disc designed by lighting tech Michael Tait that reflected beams of light around the auditorium during the intro and outro of 'CTTE'. Hardly groundbreaking stuff, but by November, it all changed when the three-dimensional fibreglass structures designed by Roger and Martyn Dean were unveiled during the *Tales from Topographic Oceans* tour. The centrepiece, which resembled a giant crab-like creature, sat above the drum riser and, when it opened, shot beams of light above the audience. For the record, although the *Topographic Oceans* tour has been much disparaged, my friends and I saw the album performed in its entirety on four separate occasions in 1973 and loved every minute of every show.

Another band whose 1973 tours were spectacular undertakings is Emerson, Lake & Palmer. The legendary *Get Me a Ladder* jaunt kicked off in Europe in February, and a tour documentary including a show in Milan in front of 50,000 Spanish fans was filmed and screened on UK TV on Boxing Day. In November, after recording *Brain Salad Surgery*, they set off across the USA and Canada with their individual names emblazoned across the roofs of three articulated trucks carrying a huge proscenium archway, Carl Palmer's mammoth stainless steel drum kit and Greg Lake's soon to become notorious Persian rug. Despite all this extravagance, smaller venues like London's legendary Marquee club

39

and the college circuit played an important role in showcasing up and coming bands. Even a reformed King Crimson consisting of seasoned musicians paid their dues at the Marquee in February 1973.

While bands like Yes and Genesis were able to reproduce their ambitious and complex arrangements, for some, what may have taken weeks of studio recording and overdubbing did not always transfer readily to the stage. In the 1970s, I witnessed several so-called legendary bands give below-par performances, not helped by poor acoustics and uncooperative PA systems. I'm also convinced that many sound engineers at the time were partially deaf, such were the painfully high volumes often endured by audiences in the name of music. I've suffered from tinnitus for many years, which I'm convinced is a result of being a regular concert-goer.

During 1973, musicians embraced technology like never before and bands lugged around increasing amounts of equipment, especially the keyboardist. The white Mellotron 400-D became synonymous with prog bands and provided a handy platform to rest a portable synth such as a Minimoog. Keith Emerson's keyboard of choice was a huge modular Moog, but he was the exception. The Minimoog is compact with a cutting edge sound that could compete with the electric guitar.

The bulky Hammond organ was still a familiar sight and some musicians even indulged in the extravagance of a grand piano. During ELP's *Brain Salad Surgery* tour, the piano would revolve 360° in the air with Emerson – the consummate showman – still playing. To vary their sound palette, guitarists and bassists would often change their instruments between – and during – songs. Steve Howe had a customised stand with the guitars mounted like the branches of a tree. Not to be outdone, the standard drum kit would often be embellished by sundry items such as gongs and tuned percussion. During his solo, Carl Palmer's party trick was to ring a ship's bell by tugging the string with his teeth.

These days, live albums appear with almost monotonous regularity, but in the 1970s, they were at a premium. Even the most popular bands averaged just one or two throughout the entire decade, so it's no wonder that bootlegs were so popular. Otherwise, milestone tours such as *Tales From Topographic Oceans*, *A Passion Play* and *The Dark Side of the Moon* would have gone undocumented. Genesis fans had to wait a full 25 years before official recordings from the *Selling England by the Pound* tour surfaced on the *Genesis Archive 1967–75* box set.

1973 itself was a particularly productive year in terms of releases. Yes, Genesis, Focus, Wishbone Ash, Uriah Heep, Hawkwind and Mahavishnu Orchestra made their live album debuts, while Traffic's *On The Road* (October) was their second. They were all well received – by fans, if not critics – and several were double – or in Yes' case triple – LPs. The Genesis and Focus recordings were edited to suit the constraints of a single LP with an absent *Supper's Ready* and a truncated *Eruption,* respectively being obvious casualties.

Thankfully, neglected live recordings from this period would later surface on reissues and box sets.

I wear My Art on My Sleeve

Songs can tell a story, music can create moods or atmospheres and, obviously, emotional responses; it can also enhance and be enhanced by images.
Roger Dean in the book *Views*, 1975.

During the 1950s and early 1960s, when the vinyl LP became the medium of choice for popular music, more often than not, the glossy but otherwise unimaginative sleeve featured a picture of the singer or group. In the late 1960s, as the music became more adventurous, then so too did the cover artwork with The Beatles' *Sgt. Pepper's Lonely Hearts Club Band* (1967) and The Who's *Tommy* (1969) being prime examples. For the first time, the artwork provided a visual interpretation of the music on the album.

With the advent of the 1970s, progressive rock bands, in particular, sought ever more fanciful artwork to adorn – and hopefully sell – the precious music they had spent many hours slavishly creating. With a few exceptions, an image of the group in question was no longer adequate, the sleeve had to provide a visual statement that both signposted and complimented the songs. The advent of the gatefold sleeve also gave independent artists and design specialists a wider canvas on which to display their artistic talents, reaching its zenith in 1973. Although the recently developed cassette tapes were very popular – and handy for recording concerts off the radio – the twelve-inch vinyl LP was still king.

Roger Dean designed his first album cover in 1968, and from 1971 onwards, he became closely associated with Yes – and although 1972 was particularly productive, his output in 1973 was prestigious. The elaborate packaging for the triple *Yessongs* album boasted four original paintings with a linking theme, while the outer sleeve for the double *Tales from Topographic Oceans* features one of his best-known illustrations. Like many of his landscape paintings, the latter includes images influenced by real locations photographed on his travels. He also designed the covers for the first two albums by Greenslade, which, like his work for Yes, included a memorable band logo and a recurring image, in this case, a many-armed hooded figure. One of his best-loved paintings, however, is for the cover of *One Live Badger*, partly because it's atypical of his more familiar otherworldly landscapes.

Like Dean, Hipgnosis designers Storm Thorgerson and Aubrey Powell had their own distinct style, designed their first sleeve in 1968 and became synonymous with one particular band, in this case, Pink Floyd. 1973 was an especially prolific year, including the sleek *The Dark Side of the Moon* gatefold with its iconic prism, which is as familiar as the songs themselves. It was one of the first covers not to include the band name or title, although my

41

1973 pressing features a sticker just in case any would-be record buyer was in doubt. Wishbone Ash's *Live Dates* is another inspired gatefold that mimics the packaging for a familiar brand of dates. Hipgnosis' designs often included photographic effects, although these were not always successful, as evidenced on the disconcerting *Houses of the Holy* sleeve for Led Zeppelin.

The artwork for ELP's *Brain Salad Surgery* was one of the most controversial of 1973 due to the sexual connotations of the title and H. R. Giger's female portrait – although the latter had been toned down for the cover. Giger would become better known as the designer of the titular creature in the *Alien* film franchise, although his gothic style is very much in evidence here. Most striking is the outer painting across two opening flaps with a porthole that opens out to reveal the inner portrait. The sleeve for the 1973 pressing of *Focus At the Rainbow* is another elaborate affair that again opens out on both sides to reveal artist Ian Beck's impression of the Moorish splendour of the Rainbow theatre's auditorium.

The distinctive record company logo on the disc itself also became synonymous with certain bands and genres. In 1972, Roger Dean was responsible for the elaborate Virgin Records logo and Harvest Records' simple but effective amoeba-like design, which played host to Pink Floyd, Barclay James Harvest and Deep Purple. Island Records' familiar and colourful art adorned records by King Crimson, Roxy Music and Emerson, Lake & Palmer prior to forming their own label Manticore in 1973. One of the most fondly remembered logos is 'The Famous Charisma Label' based on *Alice's Adventures in Wonderland* and emblazoned on records by Genesis, Van der Graaf Generator and Monty Python, amongst others. No vinyl collection would be complete without at least one from Vertigo Records whose psychedelic black and white spiral had the ability to hypnotise as Gentle Giant, Jade Warrior, or Black Sabbath spun on the turntable. Sadly, this was replaced in 1973 by an uncharacteristically uninspired design by Roger Dean.

Part 2: 20 Key Albums

In this second part of the book, twenty key albums originally released in 1973 are discussed on a track by track basis. They appear chronologically, beginning with the Mahavishnu Orchestra's *Birds of Fire* released in January and concluding with Yes' *Tales from Topographic Oceans* in December. In between, there's a varied selection of styles, including symphonic, fusion, neoclassical, space rock, avant-garde, progressive pop, Canterbury and Krautrock. Where a precise release date could not be established, I've used my judgement – and a little guesswork – in placing the album.

They are all studio recordings; live albums were initially considered but rejected on the basis that they are not wholly representative of the year in question. Commercial success did not influence the selections; some topped the charts in the UK or America while others failed to chart in any region. Two of the year's best selling albums discussed earlier are absent simply because they have been exhaustively chronicled in numerous other publications.

Thirteen of the albums are from UK acts for which I make no excuses; originality, quality and diversity was the deciding factor and not geographical location – this is not the Eurovision Song Contest, after all. For the record, the USA, Italy, France, Germany and the Netherlands are also represented.

I revisited each and every song – 135 in total – more than once and I was amazed at how well they stand up to close scrutiny nearly 50 years later. True, the albums were not all as successful as they should have been, but for the most part, they left a lasting legacy and their influence ripples through contemporary progressive rock to this day.

To remain true to the period, the bonus tracks on later reissues receive only a courtesy mention and the description of the cover artwork is based on the original vinyl sleeve. The songs on each album are listed under the headings 'side one' and 'side two' as they originally appeared on both vinyl and cassette tape in 1973.

Mahavishnu Orchestra – *Birds of Fire*

Personnel:
John McLaughlin: guitars
Rick Laird: bass
Billy Cobham: drums, percussion
Jan Hammer: keyboards, Moog, Fender Rhodes
Jerry Goodman: violin
Produced at CBS Studios, New York & Trident Studios, London by The Mahavishnu Orchestra
Recording date: August 1972
Release date: 3 January 1973
Record label: UK: CBS, USA: Columbia
Highest chart places: UK: 20, USA: 15, Australia: 38
Running time: 39:53

Although guitar virtuoso John McLaughlin was born in Doncaster, West Yorkshire – just 20 miles from where I sit writing this book – he was relatively unknown in his home country until the Mahavishnu Orchestra supported Yes at the Crystal Palace Bowl in September 1972. Dressed all in white with unfashionable – for the time – short hair and his legendary twin-necked Gibson, he certainly gave Steve Howe a run for his money that day. He already had a formidable pedigree, having performed with the likes of Alexis Korner, Georgie Fame, Jack Bruce, Tony Williams, Jimi Hendrix and Miles Davis in the 1960s.

Formed in New York in the summer of 1971, Mahavishnu Orchestra was effectively a jazz fusion supergroup comprising McLaughlin, Billy Cobham, Jan Hammer, Jerry Goodman and Rick Laird. With so many musical egos in one band, unsurprisingly, the original line-up was relatively short-lived. They disbanded at the end of 1973, with McLaughlin the only remaining member, leaving behind two studio and one live album.

The 1971 debut *The Inner Mounting Flame* drew much praise and vies with *Birds of Fire* as their most critically acclaimed album. The band that recorded the former were still relatively new, whereas the latter was conceived by a well-honed unit with many stage performances under their collective belts. By 1972, they were receiving a good deal of attention outside the USA and prog fans in Europe, in particular, sat up and took notice when *Birds of Fire* took flight at the beginning of 1973.

It was their only release to breach the UK chart where it peaked at number 20 on 31 March, not bad for an all-instrumental album. In June, they recorded a planned third album in London, but with internal tensions mounting, it was abandoned before eventually surfacing as *The Lost Trident Sessions* in September 1999. In its place, *Between Nothingness & Eternity* was released in November 1973. Recorded in New York's Central Park the previous August, it showcases the new material in a live setting.

Despite the tempestuous relationships within the band both musically and personally, the Mahavishnu Orchestra was quite simply one of the most stunning musical ensembles of the 1970s, or any other decade for that matter. Their speed and agility, at times, is jaw-dropping. In the promotional blurb printed on the original LP's inner sleeve, McLaughlin explained the rationale behind the 'Orchestra' epithet: 'We approach the music with at least the same dedication as any classical musician if not more'.

The fact that they played all instrumental music with virtuoso violinist Jerry Goodman in the ranks also added credence to the name. Much of the band's dynamics came from the interplay between guitar and violin, although all five musicians feature as soloists on the album. When the Mahavishnu Orchestra reformed in 1974, McLaughlin recruited such talents as violinist Jean-Luc Ponty and drummer Narada Michael Walden, but they never soared the same heights or burnt as brightly as the *Birds of Fire* quintet.

A non-gatefold sleeve, the cover artwork is an exotic combination of spray and brush painting with five golden 'birds of fire' – the band members? – circling below the album title. On the reverse side, spiritualist Sri Chinmoy's 1972 poem 'Revelation' includes the line 'Above the toil of life my soul Is a Bird of Fire winging the Infinite'.

Side one
'Birds of Fire' 5:41 (John McLaughlin)
Like the debut album, McLaughlin is credited with writing all the material on *Birds of Fire* which didn't sit too well with the other band members who believed that their contributions went unrecognised. Nonetheless, the title track is a stunning ensemble performance.

An intense piece, it opens with gong crashes and a swirling melange of sound from which strident violin and guitar surface. With Goodman repeating the central rhythmic motif, McLaughlin cuts loose with distorted guitar, firing a volley of notes in every direction. One night in March 1969, McLaughlin and Hendrix had jammed to the early hours and clearly, the session had paid dividends. Wringing every emotional note out of the instrument, he's supported by Laird's propulsive riff and Cobham's splashing cymbals while violin circles menacingly overhead. Only Hammer's synth seems a little lost in the melee.

Released the same year, jazz musician Don Sebesky opened his album *Giant Box* with a fourteen-minute piece that fuses 'Birds of Fire' with Igor Stravinsky's 'Firebird Suite'. It features Billy Cobham on drums and despite the disparate elements, is well worth a listen.

'Miles Beyond' (Miles Davis) 4:39 (McLaughlin)
As the title suggests, 'Miles Beyond' is dedicated to modern jazz pioneer, trumpet player and bandleader Miles Davis who McLaughlin had recorded and performed with in 1969 and 1970. On his classic album *Bitches Brew* (March 1970), Davis included the track 'John McLaughlin' in honour of the guitarist.

'Miles Beyond' opens with mellow electric piano chords, joined by drums and bass and a mighty riff from McLaughlin that Jimmy Page would have been proud of. Goodman joins the fray with exceptional bowing, but the track belongs to Cobham's explosive drumming, which fills every nook and cranny. It's a showcase for his extraordinary talents and a masterclass in precision and control.

To use that well-worn phrase, Cobham is a musician's musician. Like McLaughlin, he recorded with Miles Davis before and after the Mahavishnu Orchestra, including the legendary *Bitches Brew* album. Davis had a profound influence on his debut solo album *Spectrum* released in October 1973. A prolific solo output followed, along with guest appearances on albums by many of the great American jazz musicians.

'Celestial Terrestrial Commuters' 2:53 (McLaughlin)

Track three and Cobham is once again in the driving seat. Propelled by his inventive snare shots, the whole band lets rip, with Goodman taking the lead closely followed by Hammer's Moog pitch bending solos. Guitar and violin exchange musical blows in an extended showdown and by my estimation, it ends in a draw.

Hammer has enjoyed a successful career outside the Mahavishnu Orchestra and is best known for the synth jazz-pop hits 'Miami Vice Theme' and 'Crockett's Theme' in the 1980s.

'Sapphire Bullets of Pure Love' 0:22 (McLaughlin)

Despite the exotic title, this is a brief, almost throw away cacophony of improvisation and dissonance. The title struck a chord with American rock duo. They Might Be Giants, who purloined it for a similarly short song on their 1990 album *Flood*. It leads into...

'Thousand Island Park' 3:19 (McLaughlin)

Thousand Island Park is a beautiful lakeside location on the St. Lawrence River in New York State. No doubt, McLaughlin became familiar with the area after he relocated to America from England in 1969. The music conjures up an idyllic setting and a respite from the musical turbulence of the previous tracks.

It's a serene piano and Spanish guitar interlude maintained at a hesitant, stop-start but stately tempo. It has an almost medieval flavour with McLaughlin's rapid finger flurries worthy of the great Andrés Segovia himself. Throughout, he's matched by Hammer's fluid piano, supported by Laird's delicate and unobtrusive bass lines. Following his exhaustive contributions on the previous tracks, Cobham sits this one out.

In the 1960s, Dublin born Laird moved around the UK jazz scene and studied music before relocating to America. He passed away on 4 July 2021, five months after his 80th birthday.

'Hope' 1:55 (McLaughlin)

Closing side one of the original LP, 'Hope' is built around a repeated, ascending theme led by violin, guitar and electric piano chords. Cobham's inventive drumming once again extends beyond the rhythm – he is no mere timekeeper – before the track fades all too soon.

Although a live version of 'Hope' was recorded in Central Park in August 1973, it did not appear until 2011 on the *Unreleased Tracks from Between Nothingness & Eternity* album. It was one of five CDs in *The Complete Columbia Albums Collection* box set.

Side two
'One Word' 9:54 (McLaughlin)

On an album consisting of relatively short tracks, 'One Word' – at just shy of ten minutes – is the longest by some distance. A snare roll provides the introduction and the band hits the ground running with guitar leading the charge, supported by electric piano and a martial-like drum pattern. It eases into an extended bass solo which accelerates from moody beginnings to a frantic dash. Laird really excels himself and McLaughlin provides some uncharacteristic funky chords.

At 4:20, Goodman's bowing gets downright mean and dirty and the three-way exchanges between violin, Moog and guitar are breathtaking to the extreme. The playing is so intense that the instruments become a blur which must have kept engineer Ken Scott on his toes. Not to be outdone, at a little over the six-minute mark, Cobham weighs in with an extended drum solo and once again, his technique astounds. The rest of the band re-enter at 8:13 for a frantic, all-guns-blazing finale. A fusion in every sense of the word, all five musicians are at the top of their game and just listening to this sequence will leave you breathless.

Along with 'Hope', 'One Word' was recorded live in August 1973 and did not surface until 2011. At almost twice the length of the studio version, it was a stage regular first played in 1972 and a springboard for extended soloing and improvisation.

'Sanctuary' 5:01 (McLaughlin)

In contrast with the previous track, 'Sanctuary' is a study in mood and restraint. It's another piece the band road-tested during their extended touring in 1972. Goodman plays a melancholic theme which has a restless edge thanks to Laird and Cobham's fractured rhythm. Violin aided by guitar and delicate electric piano lifts it out of the doldrums momentarily before falling back to a languid tempo with splashing cymbals bringing it to a close.

Goodman came from a classical family background and following the Mahavishnu Orchestra, his violin talents featured on numerous film soundtracks. In 2009, he played on Dream Theater's version of 'Larks' Tongues in Aspic, Part Two', which was included on the special edition of their 2009 album *Black Clouds & Silver Linings*.

'Open Country Joy' 3:52 (McLaughlin)

Another track that displays the band's versatility, 'Open Country Joy' begins with a sweet violin theme over picked electric guitar and electric piano. After a short pause, the combined band crashes in at a little over the one minute mark. McLaughlin's guitar pyrotechnics are once again informed by Hendrix, while Goodman's restless violin and Hammer's Moog pitch-bending match him all the way.

The mood changes at 2:30 and the title becomes apparent with the appearance of a sunny, country flavoured tune. Goodman's fiddle-like bowing is exquisite, as is McLaughlin's folky guitar picking. The only thing missing is banjo, dobro and maybe a touch of pedal steel to give it that authentic country vibe. Either way, it's a pastoral delight.

'Resolution' 2:08 (McLaughlin)

The aptly titled final track 'Resolution' has a similar structure to 'Hope' that closed side one. It builds gradually from humble beginnings with a chugging guitar riff doubled by pulsating bass and an ominous drum pattern. Violin and electric piano enter to ratchet up the tension to an intense peak before the release comes with a flurry of cascading piano notes.

This is another piece that worked superbly live, proving to be an ideal set closer in 1973.

Rick Wakeman – *The Six Wives of Henry VIII*

Personnel:
Rick Wakeman: Minimoogs, 400-D Mellotrons, Steinway 9' grand piano, Hammond
C3 organ, RMI electric piano, ARP synthesiser, harpsichord, church organ,
portative organ
Additional personnel:
Bill Bruford: drums on 'Catherine of Aragon' and 'Anne Boleyn'
Ray Cooper: percussion on 'Catherine of Aragon' and 'Anne Boleyn'
Dave Cousins: electric banjo on 'Catherine Howard'
Chas Cronk: bass guitar on 'Catherine Howard'
Barry de Souza: drums on 'Catherine Howard'
Dave Lambert: guitar on 'Catherine Howard'
Mike Egan: guitar on 'Catherine of Aragon', 'Anne of Cleves', 'Anne Boleyn' and
'Catherine Parr'
Steve Howe: guitar on 'Catherine of Aragon'
Chris Squire: bass guitar on 'Catherine of Aragon'
Alan White: drums on 'Anne of Cleves', 'Jane Seymour' and 'Catherine Parr'
Dave Wintour: bass guitar on 'Anne of Cleves' and 'Catherine Parr'
Les Hurdle: bass guitar on 'Catherine of Aragon' and 'Anne Boleyn'
Frank Ricotti: percussion on 'Anne of Cleves', 'Catherine Howard' and 'Catherine Parr'
Laura Lee: vocals on 'Anne Boleyn'
Sylvia McNeill: vocals on 'Anne Boleyn'
Judy Powell: vocals on 'Catherine of Aragon'
Barry St. John: vocals on 'Catherine of Aragon'
Liza Strike: vocals on 'Catherine of Aragon' and 'Anne Boleyn'
Produced at Morgan and Trident Studios, London by Rick Wakeman
Recording date: February to October 1972
Release date: 23 January 1973
Record label: A&M
Highest chart places: UK: 7, USA: 30, Australia: 9
Running time: 36:36

In the 1970s, Rick Wakeman was a rarity – a genuine prog rock superstar. When
he joined Yes in August 1971 and departed in May 1974, both events were
front-page news in the UK music press.

In November 1971, he received a healthy advance from A&M Records during
a financially successful period with Yes, which gave him the wherewithal to
record his first solo album. Although he played on the 1971 *Piano Vibrations*
album, he was engaged as a session musician and it was one of many
recordings he contributed to at the time. The inspiration for the album came
from the book *The Private Life of Henry VIII* that Wakeman read to occupy
the in-flight hours during Yes' *Fragile* tour of the USA. The notorious 16th
century King of England and his ill-fated wives was clearly the ideal subject for
a concept album.

Lyrics were never Wakeman's strongest forte – as his later albums would testify – so he elected to record a collection of rock instrumentals which, although not unique, was considered a commercial risk at the time. The sessions were spread over a protracted eight-month period due to touring and recording commitments with Yes. In the 1978 biography *The Caped Crusader* by Dan Wooding, Wakeman confirmed:

> I would record a couple of tracks, go out on tour with Yes, and when I came back and listened to the tapes, they never sounded right. So I would do it over again and change it. It went on like that.

Although the album has that recognisable Wakeman stamp, the individual tracks are musically diverse, intended to capture the personality of each of the six queens. It was also an opportunity to exploit the array of keyboards he had at his fingertips. He makes few concessions to Renaissance music or the instrumentation of the period; instead, it's six musical portraits in a 20th-century setting. Amongst an arsenal of analogue keyboards, the Minimoog features prominently and was many keyboardists' lead instrument of choice in the early 1970s. Wisely, Rick engaged the services of musicians he was familiar with, including members of Yes, Strawbs and a host of session players and vocalists. Conscious not to sound like a surrogate Yes album, his then-current bandmates are sparingly deployed.

A piece was written for Henry, but it was omitted from the album due to the constraints of vinyl. Titled 'Defender of the Faith', It eventually surfaced on the 2009 live recording *The Six Wives of Henry VIII Live at Hampton Court Palace*. Not yet a solo touring musician in 1972, Rick featured short extracts from the album in his solo spot during Yes' *Close to the Edge* tour. It's included on *Yessongs* under the title 'Excerpts from The Six Wives of Henry VIII'.

The Six Wives launched Rick's solo career, and nearly 50 years on, he has a staggering 80 studio albums to his credit, making him a contender for the most prolific prog artist of all time. He was also an inspiration for other musicians – particularly his Yes colleagues – to flex their musical muscles outside the confines of a band environment.

To add a note of levity to the otherwise serious subject, the cover artwork features a sepia-tinged photo of Rick striding past waxwork models of Henry and his wives on display at London's Madame Tussauds. On the back of the gatefold, there is a portrait of each wife accompanied by biographical notes, while the inside spread features a studio photo of Wakeman encircled by his keyboard rig.

Side one
'Catherine of Aragon' 3:45 (Rick Wakeman)
The opening track began life as 'Handle with Care', which Wakeman had intended as his debut offering for Yes' *Fragile* album in 1971. This was nixed

by A&M and so it was reworked for this album. Appropriately, given the track's origins, Steve Howe, Chris Squire and Bill Bruford lend their collective talents to 'Catherine of Aragon'. She was Henry's first wife and, by all accounts, had more brains than beauty but it was her shrewdness that kept her head on her shoulders, unlike some of her successors.

Organ, guitar and piano make a dramatic entrance before the latter takes up the memorable main theme, underpinned by articulate bass and Ray Cooper's thunderous timpani rolls. Bruford's drumming is a tad low in the mix and he's absent from the next section, which features ambient synth followed by Wakeman's trademark rhapsodic piano. He's accompanied by acoustic guitar and a wordless female choir which builds to an epic peak. A brief flourish of piano before organ, bass and drums return to bring the track to a triumphant conclusion.

'Catherine of Aragon' is a perfect album opener and was regularly performed by Wakeman with The English Rock Ensemble in subsequent years and occasionally paired with 'Catherine Howard'.

'Anne of Cleves' 7:50 (Wakeman)

Wife number four Anne of Cleves was divorced soon after her marriage to make way for Catherine Howard, but fortunately – like Catherine of Aragon – she evaded the axeman. The track's freeform, jazz-fusion style, in Rick's opinion, reflected Anne's mental state.

A spiralling electric piano motif opens proceedings before launching into a frantic organ-led jam fest that dominates this near eight-minute piece. Rick indulges in some jazzy noodling and improvisation, supported by the stunning rhythm partnership of Dave Wintour (bass), Alan White (drums) and Frank Ricotti (hand toms).

Along the way, there are subliminal nods to The Hollies' 1966 hit 'Bus Stop' penned by Graham Gouldman and, more overtly, the Latin jazz standard 'El Cumbanchero' written by Puerto Rican Rafael Hernández Marín in the 1940s. They appear at 1:40 and 3:30, respectively. At 4:12, a synth fanfare, harpsichord break and swirling electronics are thrown into the mix before picking up from where it left off. Crashing piano chords and Mike Egan's dissonant guitar solo have the final word before the whole thing finally runs out of steam. White's muscular drumming is fantastic on this track and his first studio recording after joining Yes.

'Catherine Howard' 6:36 (Wakeman)

The free-spirited Catherine Howard was much favoured by Henry, but when he found out about her extramarital indiscretions, she was beheaded in 1542. Nonetheless, she is favoured with the strongest melody and probably the album's best-known piece. A week before the album hit the shops, it was performed – or rather mimed to – by Wakeman and friends on BBC TV's late-night rock show, *The Old Grey Whistle Test*, on 16 January 1973. 'Catherine

Howard' became a stage favourite in later years for The English Rock Ensemble and was performed during the *Wakeman With Wakeman* tours in the early 1990s.

Solo piano, swiftly joined by drums, bass, acoustic guitar and Mellotron, introduces the main theme, which is then recapitulated in several different settings. Dave Cousins' tranquil electric banjo solo provides a respite before being overwhelmed by a strident Moog fanfare. At 2:55, it morphs into honky-tonk piano mode – which would become another Wakeman trademark – followed by a burst of Hammond, piano and Mellotron stabs. The main melody returns, played by Mellotron strings, supported by piano arpeggios and tubular bells. The haunting final sequence at 5:50 with Mellotron flute picking up the main circular theme is heavenly and is repeated during the slow fade.

Side two
'Jane Seymour' 4:46 (Wakeman)

Henry's third wife, Jane Seymour, opens side two of the original vinyl LP. She had a passive nature and gave him the son he so desperately desired, but the birth resulted in her own death, aged just 28.

Electric organs at the time were unable to reproduce the celestial sound Rick was looking for on this track, and he was granted permission to record the huge pipe organ at St Giles Church, Cripplegate, London. The majestic tone provides the perfect leitmotif for this gentlest of ladies.

The mood is broken at 2:45 and 3:10 with irreverent Moog stabs. Interviewed on *The Old Grey Whistle Test* in 1972, Rick claimed that the church organ and synth represented the diverse aspects of Jane Seymour's personality, who had an old head on her shoulders but died young. I'm not convinced, but nearly 50 years on, the track wouldn't sound right any other way.

This is another occasional live piece that has been performed solo, with The English Rock Ensemble and with an orchestra – most notably at London's Hampton Court Palace in May 2009.

'Anne Boleyn (The Day Thou Gavest Lord Hath Ended)' 6:32 (Wakeman, E. J. Hopkins)

This penultimate piece alternates between fast and slow passages with fine drum support. It begins with a touch of airy piano before hitting its hyperactive stride driven by synth and organ. The rich tones of the choir enter at 2:03, followed by a joyous piano-led theme that introduces two very different synth solos. The first sounds almost funky, while the second adopts a higher-pitched timbre. As more instruments join in, it develops into a jazz-fusion workout before galloping piano and organ enter the fray and spiral skywards.

When Henry married his second wife, he unreasonably demanded a son, not the daughter Anne Boleyn gave birth to. Her reward for this, and her fiery temper, was execution in May 1536.

The mood changes at 5:30 with a poignant version of 'St Clement' – the music for the hymn, 'The Day Thou Gavest Lord Hath Ended' – on grand piano. A subdued choir provides the sublime backing, bringing the track to a calming conclusion. Rick was inspired to add 'St Clement' after he recorded the track and then dreamt that same night that he heard the hymn playing at Anne Boleyn's funeral service.

'Catherine Parr' 7:00 (Wakeman)

The final track is appropriately dedicated to the sixth wife, Catherine Parr. She was level headed and outlived Henry but died after bearing a child to her fourth husband, Thomas Seymour.

This is a multi-part gem containing no less than eight separate sequences. On 18 January 1974, when Rick unveiled *Journey to the Centre of the Earth* at London's Royal Festival Hall, 'Catherine Parr' – along with 'Catherine Howard' and 'Anne Boleyn' – was performed in the first half of the set.

A galloping organ theme sets the scene with an almost country and western groove. Rick's dexterous playing, Dave Wintour's lead bass lines and Alan White's drumming is a powerful combination and a joy to behold. In a punchy staccato section, Mellotron provides the choir and combines with piano for the haunting sequence that follows. At the three minute mark, it hits its rock stride with a rhythmic Moog theme that glides into a tubular bells section.

An ambient interlude with skyrocketing electronic effects and celestial organ is swept away by the simulated sounds of crashing waves. The opening, uplifting organ theme is reprised, joined by double-tracked Moogs which become more dominant before the glorious sound of the Hammond C3 and rotating Leslie speaker brings the track and album to a close.

Greenslade – *Greenslade*

Personnel:
Dave Greenslade: keyboards
Dave Lawson: keyboards, vocals
Tony Reeves: bass guitar, double bass
Andrew McCulloch: drums, percussion
Produced at Morgan Studios, London by Tony Reeves, Dave Greenslade & Stuart Taylor
Recording date: Completed December 1972
Release date: February 1973
Record label: Warner Bros.
Highest chart places: UK: Did not chart, USA: Did not chart
Running time: 40:34

There was never any doubt that Greenslade would be on the shortlist for this section of the book; the hard part was deciding which album to choose. This eponymous debut was the first of two studio releases in 1973 with the similarly excellent *Bedside Manners Are Extra* following in November. On balance, *Greenslade* just has the edge, in my opinion, still sounding fresh and vital nearly 50 years on. Undeservedly, neither album charted in the UK, although it wasn't for lack of promotion. They appeared on BBC TV's *The Old Grey Whistle Test* and I caught them on tour in 1973. Imagine my surprise when five minutes before they were due on stage, I found myself standing next to Dave Greenslade in the men's toilets. Needless to say, I didn't feel it was an appropriate time or place to ask for his autograph.

Formed the previous year by four musicians with a solid background in jazz-rock and prog, Greenslade swiftly developed into a formidable ensemble. Their line-up was unique at the time – even by prog rock standards – featuring two keyboardists – Dave Greenslade and Dave Lawson – and no lead guitarist. Greenslade plays Hammond organ, Mellotron and piano while Lawson handles synth, electric piano and is also responsible for the lyrics and vocals.

Dave Greenslade's CV included British jazz-rockers Colosseum – along with Tony Reeves – and the band If. Dave Lawson's grounding included stints with The Alan Bown Set and Web. Like Chris Squire and Jon Camp of Renaissance, Tony Reeves had an impressive bass technique, often playing lead lines, even solos. Andrew McCulloch's pedigree included Manfred Mann, King Crimson and the trio Fields, who released a shamefully overlooked self-titled album in 1971.

The third Greenslade album *Spyglass Guest* (1974), was their best selling, spending three weeks in the chart, peaking at 34. It featured six-string guitar, as did the final album *Time and Tide* (1975). They are both very fine releases – especially the latter – but it didn't prevent Greenslade from disbanding in 1976. Dave Greenslade turned his attention to solo releases and TV themes, Lawson became a highly respected session musician in the world of movie scores, Reeves joined Curved Air for a spell and McCulloch eventually retired from the music business.

Despite the individual members' successes elsewhere, it's fair to surmise that Greenslade was the pinnacle of their artistic careers. Dave Greenslade and Reeves reformed the band in the early 2000s, but the studio album *Large Afternoon* failed to capture the magic of their earlier recordings. *Live 2001 – The Full Edition* fared better, but the band folded soon after.

The album artwork is one of Roger Dean's most evocative, with a logo as distinctive as the one he designed for Yes. The multiple-armed hooded magician was possibly inspired by Hindu statues and was reprised by Dean for the cover of *Bedside Manners Are Extra*. He was also responsible for the stylised typography on the inner lyric sheet and both covers feature his signature marbling technique. The magician also provided the backdrop for Greenslade's stage set and returned for the covers of *Time and Tide*, *Large Afternoon* (2000) and Dave Greenslade's debut solo album *Cactus Choir* (1976), although Dean only participated in the latter.

Side one
'Feathered Friends' 6:47 (Dave Greenslade, Dave Lawson)
This is a humdinger of an opener that lyrically cuts to the chase. As the title implies, it's a song with an ecological message of the 'what are they doing to the planet' variety. The opening lines 'What's your poison? Well, here's mud in your eye' are typical of Lawson's penchant for double meaning wordplay. His distinct vocals are very much an acquired taste and quite intense at times. There's no denying the passion in his delivery, however, and this song, in particular, tests the upper limits of his vocal range.

The instrumental intro driven by fuzzed organ rocks along at a lively pace. Lawson's vocals enter at 1:19, supported by organ, piano and agile bass and drums. The vocal melody is wistful and engaging, but the song's ace card is dealt at 4:12 – a majestic Mellotron strings arrangement of the melody that still has the power to send shivers down the spine.

Despite their jazz backgrounds, it's evident from this opening track that the band embraced symphonic rock with the emphasis on melody and ensemble performance rather than indulgent soloing. Unsurprisingly, 'Feathered Friends' quickly became a live favourite and was resurrected for the 2001 tour after the band reformed. Warner Bros. also released 'Feathered Friends' as a promo single in 1973 with the album's two shortest songs, 'An English Western' and 'Temple Song' on the flip side.

'An English Western' 3:27 (Greenslade)
Lawson gives his vocal cords a rest for this exuberant, upbeat instrumental, but his piano playing is suitably robust. He's matched by Greenslade's superb organ flights while McCulloch's busy drumming is everywhere. It certainly has a vaguely western feel, bringing to mind those catchy cowboy film themes by

the likes of Elmer Bernstein and Jerome Moross in the late 1950s and early 1960s. There's also a touch of Aaron Copland in the dancing midsection. All too soon, a short burst of Mellotron strings announces the end.

'An English Western' is another piece that went down well live, often with an extended mid-section.

'Drowning Man' 5:50 (Greenslade)

Dave Greenslade was responsible for the lyrics to this song which boasts Lawson's finest singing on the album. Based around a repeated verse and chorus, it's possibly the final thoughts of a dying soldier on the battlefield. In the moody intro, the double-tracked vocal harmonies are sumptuous with an authentic Beach Boys vibe. At 1:55, it breaks into a gallop with Mellotron, organ and electric piano leading a merry dance.

At the halfway mark, it goes all funky with fazed electric piano and a syncopated rhythm before a drum roll and Mellotron crescendo heralds a return to the opening song. The Leslie speaker bounces the Hammond between the left and right channels and a lovely recapitulation of the vocal melody with soaring strings provides a fitting finale.

'Drowning Man' was regularly performed live between 1973 and 1974, but by 1975, it had given way to songs from *Spyglass Guest* and *Time and Tide*.

'Temple Song' 3:34 (Greenslade, Lawson)

Bookended by three songs on either side, this delicate meditation is the album's centrepiece, providing a sublime contrast. It has overtones of oriental music, thanks to tuned percussion, cymbal rides and rhythmic electric piano picking out the slight melody. The subtle lead bass lines complement Lawson's restrained vocal and the delightful two-verse, one-chorus lyrics. The opening line – 'See the sundance in the temple' – references the album's closing track. A heavenly outro of Mellotron flute and wordless harmonies brings side one to a calming close.

Released in May 1973, 'Temple Song' was the band's first commercially available single, but unsurprisingly, it proved to be unlikely chart material. 'An English Western' provided the B side.

Side two
'Melange' 7:30 (Tony Reeves, Greenslade, Lawson)

Launching side two in style, 'Melange' is out of the starting gates like a thoroughbred, with Reeves' powerful bass punctuations supported by Mellotron. From here on in, it's a tour de force performance by the bassist, with no less than four separate solos. The first is superb, underscored by Mellotron, while at the two-minute mark, the second is tonally very different but equally brilliant, overlaid with harmonious wordless vocals.

At 3:22, things really begin to heat up with Reeves – unaccompanied to begin with – joined by sparse piano and hi-hat. A drum roll at 4:49 announces the album's pièce de résistance with monumental bass lines accompanied by fuzzed organ and Mellotron. It builds to an epic peak and a stirring, quasi-symphonic finale with magnificent drum fills.

If there was ever any concern that the band were compromised by the absence of six-string guitar, Reeves laid such doubts to rest with this instrumental, the album's crowning glory in the author's opinion.

'What Are You Doing to Me' 4:44 (Lawson)

Now that I've got the hyperbole out of my system, this is a more measured critique of the penultimate track. It's the only song where Lawson is responsible for the music as well as the punning lyrics and it's possibly my least favourite, although the two are not necessarily connected. The angst-ridden, wall to wall singing doesn't do it any favours, however.

It certainly rocks along at a lively pace, relating the story of love gone wrong thanks to infidelity on the part of the protagonist's partner. The grandiose instrumental bridge that occurs twice in the song sounds a tad out of place but is welcome nonetheless with its striking chord progressions. Intentionally or not, tip-toeing electric piano at the end suggests the song's broken-hearted protagonist is finally heading for the door.

'Sundance' 8:45 (Greenslade)

The closing instrumental is another fan favourite and was regularly performed live in 1973 and 1974. Like 'Feathered Friends', it made a welcome return to the stage in 2001. With the best part of nine minutes at its disposal, the solo piano opening takes its time and the delicate melody is minimalist but gorgeous. It soon hits its jazz-funk stride with busy drumming filling every inch – or centimetre if you prefer – of the track. A galloping drum and organ sequence follows, underpinned by Mellotron strings. Maintaining the mood, bouncing synth notes herald a jam section with improvised organ soloing over-energetic bass and drums.

This is the closest the album comes to jazz fusion territory and it was an opportunity for the band to demonstrate their chops when played live. A wave of Mellotron strings at 4:55 announces a change of key and tempo before accelerating into a rampant jam sequence. The main theme is reprised, only this time with more punch and drive. It subsides at 7:34 for a tranquil return to the acoustic piano melody doubled by bass before Mellotron flute has the final word – or eight seconds at least.

King Crimson – *Larks' Tongues in Aspic*

Personnel:
Robert Fripp: electric and acoustic guitars, Mellotron, Hohner pianet, devices
John Wetton: bass, vocals, piano on 'Exiles'
Bill Bruford: drums, timbales, cowbell, wood block
David Cross: violin, viola, Mellotron, Hohner pianet, flute on 'Exiles'
Jamie Muir: percussion, drums, allsorts
Produced at Command Studios, London by King Crimson
Recording date: January and February 1973
Release date: 23 March 1973
Record label: Island
Highest chart places: UK: 20, USA: 61, Canada: 56
Running time: 46:36

Guitarist extraordinaire Robert Fripp could never be accused of musical complacency or wallowing in past glories. He co-founded King Crimson in 1968 and following the departure of Ian McDonald, Michael Giles and eventually Greg Lake, he assumed sole leadership in 1970. Following four studio and one live album, he deconstructed the band in 1972 and rebuilt it from the ground up. Drummer Bill Bruford – who was seeking an outlet to express his jazz aspirations away from the strict regime of Yes – was recruited in July 1972, joined by percussionist Jamie Muir, violinist David Cross and bassist John Wetton fresh from Family.

Like Fripp and Lake, the early part of Wetton's career had been spent in Dorset around the south coast of England. Cross was relatively unknown, but he was an inspired choice, being a perfect foil for Fripp's stinging guitar style. Muir came from a free jazz background and was responsible for the album title, a spontaneous response after listening to a playback of one of the tracks. 'Spontaneous' is also an apt description for his wild performances on stage.

It was evident that the new Crimson was going to be a liberating experience and a radical musical departure with formal musical structures, balanced by lengthy improvisation and free jazz techniques, anchored by Wetton's articulate vocal melodies. He was a natural successor to Greg Lake, and stepping into the shoes of Pete Sinfield was lyricist Richard Palmer-James who played in several 1960s bands with a young Wetton and co-founded Supertramp in 1970. Although Wetton would later develop into a fine wordsmith, here Palmer-James literally put the words into his mouth. In the *Yesyears* video, Bill Bruford confirmed that: 'We perceived of ourselves as a kind of improvising rock group really, in a European sense'. He also observed that: 'And Robert, he has a dark side certainly, and that resonated within the band.'

The first group rehearsal was on 4 September 1972, followed by four warm-up shows in Germany in October and a 28-date tour of the UK in November and December. This gave the band the opportunity to work up the material on the road prior to going into the studio. The five-piece line-up was short-lived, however; following recording sessions for the album, Muir played his final Crimson gig at London's Marquee club on 10 February 1973.

When I saw the band perform as a quartet at Leicester University in October 1973, they were a revelation. Fripp was totally absorbed in his guitar noodling and barely acknowledged the audience, Bruford hit everything in sight, Cross' playing dazzled and Wetton proved to be a professional if self-conscious frontman. The music was bold and challenging and often bore little resemblance to the recorded material. If America had the Mahavishnu Orchestra – albeit fronted by a Brit – the UK had the equivalent in King Crimson.

Larks' Tongues in Aspic was enthusiastically received by fans and critics alike, as were its two successors, *Starless and Bible Black* and *Red* (both 1974), although for the latter, they were reduced to a trio of Fripp, Bruford, and Wetton. Fripp was known for his unpredictability, but it still took everyone by surprise when in late 1974, he announced the band was no more and this time it was for good. Fortunately, he was only half right but even so, with the exception of the 1975 live album *USA*, it would be the last murmur from Crimson for more than six years.

When the band reformed in 1981, only Fripp and Bruford returned from the previous incarnation. Wetton would go on to become one of prog rock's most seasoned journeymen with a CV that included Uriah Heep, Roxy Music, Wishbone Ash, U.K. – with Bill Bruford – and most notably, fronting prog-AOR superband Asia.

The cover artwork for *Larks' Tongues in Aspic* is minimalist but very effective, featuring the image of a blazing sun with a benign face against a white background. Like several of the previous King Crimson albums, there's no band name or album title to distract from the tasteful design.

Side one
'Larks' Tongues in Aspic, Part One' 13:36 (David Cross, Robert Fripp, John Wetton, Bill Bruford, Jamie Muir)

The album and part one of the title instrumental opens with the gentle sound of tuned percussion, rippling like a gentle stream on a summer's day. It's the lull before the storm, however. Distorted guitar and insistent violin enter around the three-minute mark before the whole band comes crashing in, and they mean business. Five minutes in and our ears are assailed with a disjointed and very complex sequence with restless guitar chords supported by unearthly percussion. Around the midway point, Wetton demonstrates his bass chops with a blistering solo supported by crashing – and very high in the mix – percussion. Just listening to this track, one can easily visualise Muir flailing his arms like a whirling dervish.

Like many of the instrumental set pieces on the album, Fripp was mostly responsible for the framework, allowing the rest of the band to develop their parts and fill in the gaps. Wetton later likened it to completing a musical jigsaw puzzle.

At 7:40, the mayhem subsides for a mournful and unaccompanied violin solo. Although it sounds mostly improvised, a sweet melody begins to develop, joined by subtle oriental flavoured percussion at 11:00. Supported by rhythm guitar and drums, it builds to a crescendo and a stunning but all too short lead bass theme underscored by violin before playing out as it began.

Phew, it's only the first track and already it's been a draining listening experience. It has been performed live many times over the years by different incarnations of the band who have put their own individual spin on it. The bare bones of the piece date back to a jazzy instrumental called 'A Peacemaking Stint Unrolls', which was recorded in October 1971 – but not released at the time – by the Robert Fripp, Mel Collins, Ian Wallace and Boz Burrell line-up.

'Book of Saturday' 2:49 (Fripp, Wetton, Richard Palmer-James)

As a respite to the lengthy opening instrumental, the rest of side-one on the original vinyl LP is given over to two relatively melodic songs that hark back to earlier days. Fripp's graceful guitar picking is not too dissimilar to the hook in Spandau Ballet's mega-hit 'True' released ten years later. Instead of Tony Hadley, we are greeted by Wetton's warm vocal tones. It was his first outing as a lead singer and he certainly makes his mark. At less than three minutes, he has just enough time to deliver Palmer-James' elaborate story in four verses. It tells of a complex relationship that he neither has the strength nor desire to break away from. In my interpretation, the 'book' is essentially memories, both good and bad. A touch of lyrical violin is the only other ingredient needed for this blissful exercise in harmony and restraint.

'Exiles' 7:40 (Cross, Fripp, Palmer-James)

Disorientating sounds and electronic effects prevail before the mood is broken around the two-minute mark with the musical equivalent of a relaxed Sunday afternoon stroll in the park. Wetton's mellow vocal is backed by lush violin and Bruford's shuffle drum pattern, a nostalgic throwback to Michael Giles' trademark style on *In the Court of the Crimson King*. To enhance the effect, Mellotron strings sway gently in the background and later, a touch of gentle piano and guitar. Wetton's vocal performance is a masterclass in warmth and restraint throughout, although the lyrics are quite personal to Palmer-James. They reflect the solitary experience of being a stranger in a strange land and thoughts of friends and loved ones left behind.

Just when it seems like we're heading for a slow fade, at 7:05, It rises to a glorious crescendo that recalls the intro to 'Epitaph' in all its magnificent glory. Comparisons with King Crimson's 1969 works are not surprising given that 'Exiles' borrows from an unrecorded piece titled 'Mantra', which the band performed around this period. 'Exiles' itself would become an established stage favourite and along with 'Easy Money' and 'Larks' Tongues in Aspic, Part Two', it appeared on the live album *USA*, recorded in June 1974 and released in May 1975.

Side two

'Easy Money' 7:54 (Fripp, Wetton, Palmer-James)

For newcomers to the album, side two starts surprisingly with a loud, plodding rhythm that's very close to the 1970 novelty hit 'Neanderthal Man' by Hotlegs – later known as 10cc – which is not intended as an insult. Forgoing the 'I am Neanderthal man' chant, Wetton opts for a wordless vocal chant instead. A syncopated rhythm and a touch of distorted guitar support the verses before the familiar short chorus erupts at regular intervals.

In the improvised instrumental bridge, you can sense that band feeling their way, exploring the limitless possibilities open to this talented quintet. Only Bruford's measured drumming and Wetton's bass lines provide a semblance of order. Encouraged by Muir, Bruford cuts loose just as the jarring vocal melody returns. The manic laugh at the end sums up the mood of the song perfectly, which criticises the capitalist, money-grabbing side of the entertainment business. Unsurprisingly, 'Easy Money' is another song that works well live and is often extended to around the ten-minute mark.

'The Talking Drum' 7:26 (Cross, Fripp, Wetton, Bruford, Muir)

The penultimate track and another low key beginning. Almost until the halfway mark, little seems to be happening in this instrumental save for ambient sounds and percussion loops. Out of the darkness, violin emerges underpinned by a steady rhythm that has a touch of early Pink Floyd about it. The violin is supported by what sounds like a flute until all becomes clear around the five-minute mark when it turns out to be an eerily toned guitar. Throughout, Bruford and Wetton maintain a rock-solid beat while violin goes into overdrive, reaching an ear-piercing crescendo. Like many of the album's offerings, 'The Talking Drum' would enjoy a long life in the band's setlist.

'Larks' Tongues in Aspic, Part Two' 7:12 (Fripp)

Fripp takes sole writing credit for the closing instrumental and it's his angular, staccato riff that gets things underway and maintains a constant presence throughout, underpinned by precision bass and drums. Steve Hackett was influenced by King Crimson and, two years later, he released something very similar in the shape of 'A Tower Struck Down' on his solo debut album, *Voyage of the Acolyte*. The mood and tempo take several less intense diversions but always returns to the same incessant riff. If Fripp was influenced by classical music in any way, then the shifting dynamics and rhythmic twists suggest Béla Bartók as the prime mover.

At four minutes, Cross' violin solo almost screams in agony and things get even more intense if that's possible, driven by Bruford's phenomenal drumming. Not for the first time on the album, the eventual release comes in the form of an extended crescendo followed by a final fade.

Like its namesake that opened the album, this remained a popular stage number well into the 21st century. The heavy beat and jagged riffs were not lost on prog-metallers Dream Theater, who released their version of 'Larks' Tongues in Aspic, Part Two' in 2009. It's a worthy version, especially the symphonic embellishments.

Gong – *Flying Teapot*

Personnel:
Daevid Allen (Dingo Virgin): vocals, guitar
Gilli Smyth (The Good Witch Yoni): space whisper
Tim Blake (Hi T Moonweed the favourite): synthesizer, vocals
Didier Malherbe (The Good Count Bloomdido Bad De Grasse): saxes, flute
Steve Hillage (Stevie Hillside): guitar
Christian Tritsch (The Submarine Captain): guitar
Francis Moze (Francis Bacon): bass guitar, piano
Laurie Allan (Lawrence the alien): drums
Rachid Houari (Rachid Whoarewe the Treeclimber): congas
Produced at The Manor Studios, Oxfordshire, England by Giorgio Gomelsky
Recording date: January 1973
Release date: 25 May 1973
Record label: Virgin
Highest chart places: UK: Did not chart, USA: Did not chart
Running time: 39:45

Flying Teapot – AKA *Radio Gnome Invisible Part 1* – shares the same release date and record label as *Tubular Bells* and was recorded in the same studio by the same engineers, but there the similarities end. Gong's quirky concept was never destined to inflate Virgin Records' bank balance in the same way that Mike Oldfield's masterwork did. In fact, none of the band's records achieved chart success in the UK, or most anywhere else for that matter. Gong are quite possibly the ultimate cult band; in fact, the term could have been invented with them in mind.

Flying Teapot was the first of two albums in 1973 from this Anglo-French collective and as with Greenslade, it was a tough call for the author in deciding which one to include in this section. The follow-up *Angels Egg* (December) is another fan favourite and received a modicum of chart success in Australia from where band leader Daevid Allen originated. Together with *You* (1974), they make up the 'Radio Gnome Invisible' trilogy, Gong's most popular period. Critics were equally smitten; although bands like Jethro Tull, Yes and ELP were lambasted for self-indulgence in 1973, Gong could seemingly do no wrong.

A veteran of the Canterbury scene, Allen pieced the band together in 1967 and due to the increasing number of musicians involved with each album, they went through more lineup changes than almost any band I can recall. Guitar supremo Steve Hillage was one of five new arrivals to climb on board for *Flying Teapot*. Each band member was given a nonsensical alias by Allen, which appeared in the album credits (as reproduced above in brackets).

At the heart of the album are Allen's surreal storytelling and eccentric brand of humour, which is a throwback to the hippy-trippy era of the mid to late 1960s, informed by the Goons by way of The Beatles' *Yellow Submarine*. It introduces the protagonist, Zero the Hero, who has a close encounter with

63

the Pot Head Pixies who travel to earth in a flying teapot to spread their message of enlightenment. The lyrics don't bear close examination – unless you're on Allen's wavelength, that is – and the allusion to cannabis smoking is indicative of his recreational habits at the time. Musically, it's not a million miles from Frank Zappa's work with the Mothers of Invention. In many cases, the vocals are treated like another instrument and often used for their textured, rhythmic quality.

Such is the enduring popularity of *Flying Teapot* amongst Gong aficionados, virtually every song on the album has been performed live in one shape or another over the ensuing decades. It remains prog's answer to *The Rocky Horror Picture Show*, despite Allen's untimely demise in March 2015.

Gong were one of several bands that appeared on the infamous double live LP *Greasy Truckers Live At Dingwalls Dance Hall* recorded in October 1973. Also on the bill were Camel, Henry Cow, and the Global Village Trucking Company and although the event was staged in London, bizarrely, Gong's two contributions were recorded in Tabarka, Tunisia and the less exotic Sheffield, South Yorkshire.

Allen is responsible for the cover artwork which has a naive charm and resembles something out of a children's cartoon. The inside of the gatefold sleeve contains more of his drawings and doodles and references 'The Pocket History of the Planet Gong'.

Side one
'Radio Gnome Invisible' 5:33 (Daevid Allen)
Following spacey effects and what sounds like someone making blowing noises with their mouth, the song begins in earnest with heavy chords, a staccato saxophone riff and a strident marching rhythm. Allen's pronounced singing is drenched in reverb and when male and female vocals combine, the nonsensical words are accompanied by a Russian-Yiddish folk melody. The midway bridge sees a return to spacey drones and distant voices before developing into a sax driven segment ripe with melodrama that would be right at home in a theatrical stage musical. Towards the end, the repeated choral hook 'Radio Gnome Invisible' is treated to a distinct French accent before the song turns full circle and plays out as it began.

'Flying Teapot' 12:30 (Allen, Francis Moze)
The title track is one of Gong's longest, especially the original vinyl version – discussed here – which is 37 seconds longer than the reissued CD version. The low key intro of ambient sounds, ethereal voices, more cosmic effects, a hint of flute and improvised sax wouldn't be out of place on a horror or sci-fi movie soundtrack. It's very reminiscent of Jerry Goldsmith's atmospheric score for *Alien* in 1979. At 2:20, a polyrhythmic juxtaposition of sprightly bass and a skipping drum pattern moves along at a brisk pace overlaid by scat vocals and rhythmic sax. The section that follows has a breezy jazz-funk vibe with some

Right: With *Dark Side of the Moon,* Roger Waters (second from right) began to assert his control over Pink Floyd.

Left: Bass guitar was just one of many instruments Mike Oldfield played on the groundbreaking *Tubular Bells.*

Right: Although no studio albums were released in 1973, it was Dutch quartet Focus' most successful year.

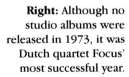

Left: The colourful cover artwork for *Birds of Fire* reflects the quality of the music contained within. (*Columbia*)

Right: Rick Wakeman gatecrashes an Elizabethan family portrait for the cover of *The Six Wives of Henry VIII*. (*A&M*)

Left: The cover of Greenslade's debut album was just one of several imaginative designs by Roger Dean in 1973. (*Warner Bros*)

Right: The tastefully understated cover for *Larks' Tongues in Aspic* gave little indication of the sonic assault that King Crimson had in store for the unwary listener. *(Island)*

Left: With a global oil crisis and fuel rationing in 1973, a *Flying Teapot* was the only way to travel. *(Virgin)*

Right: The fictional planets Felona and Sorona are represented by the female and male figures on the cover of Le Orme's fourth album. *(Charisma)*

Left: The incomparable Mahavishnu Orchestra in full flight during a recording for BBC television.

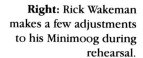

Right: Rick Wakeman makes a few adjustments to his Minimoog during rehearsal.

Left: Looking pleased with their efforts, Greenslade produced two excellent studio albums in 1973.

Right: Percussionist Jamie Muir left King Crimson shortly after the release of *Larks' Tongues in Aspic,* which explains his absence from this photoshoot.

Left: Looking more like a hippy commune than a band, Gong attempt to communicate telepathically with frontman extraordinaire Daevid Allen.

Right: Sitting on the causeway, Le Orme contemplate the fate of the fictional planets Felona and Sorona.

Above: With flute in hand, a typically animated Ian Anderson puts Jethro Tull through their paces in 1973.

Right: The five-piece Can desperately in need of a bigger stage.

Left: Kayak's casual dress sense is in stark contrast to the glam rock look they adopted for promotional purposes in 1974.

Above: Gentle Giant looking mean, moody and magnificent in this 1973 press photo for *In A Glass House.*

Left: Despite success in Europe and America, Premiata Forneria Marconi found themselves on the breadline in the early 1970s.

Right: A 1973 publicity photo of Renaissance to promote the newly released *Ashes Are Burning.* From left to right, Terry Sullivan, Annie Haslam, Jon Camp and John Tout.

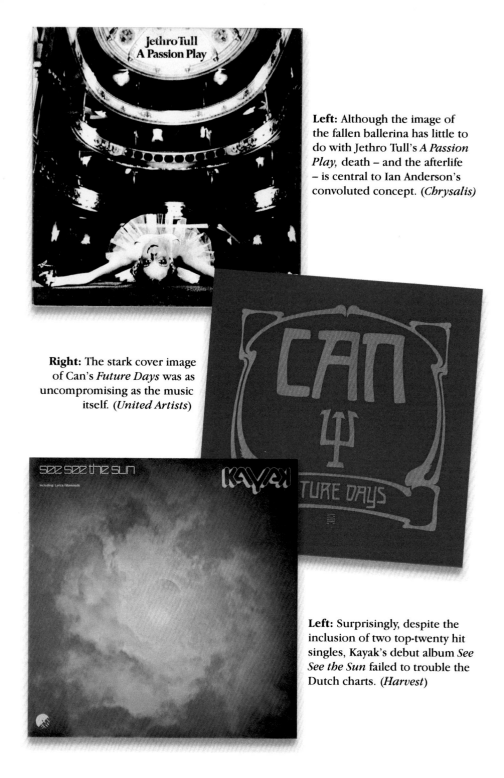

Left: Although the image of the fallen ballerina has little to do with Jethro Tull's *A Passion Play,* death – and the afterlife – is central to Ian Anderson's convoluted concept. (*Chrysalis*)

Right: The stark cover image of Can's *Future Days* was as uncompromising as the music itself. (*United Artists*)

Left: Surprisingly, despite the inclusion of two top-twenty hit singles, Kayak's debut album *See See the Sun* failed to trouble the Dutch charts. (*Harvest*)

Right: Although the cover artwork is in black and white, the music on Gentle Giant's fifth album *In a Glass House* is as colourful as any of their other 1970s releases. (*Vertigo*)

Left: The pastoral artwork for Premiata Forneria Marconi's debut English album *Photos of Ghosts* was a radical departure from the surreal images on their Italian album covers. (*Manticore*)

Right: One half of Renaissance, Annie Haslam and Terence Sullivan adopt a more serious pose for the cover of the American release of *Ashes Are Burning*. (*Sovereign*)

Above: Caravan have every right to look confident; they are the quintessential Canterbury band.

Below: Although they often disagreed (including which direction to look for this photo), for many fans, this is the definitive Genesis line-up.

Left: Conveniently posing in name order from left to right, Emerson, Lake and Palmer.

Below: Nektar in 1973 preempt the 'young men with bushy beards' fashion statement of more recent times.

Left: It was necessary to open out the gatefold sleeve to reveal the full title of *For Girls Who Grow Plump in the Night*, and the significance of the cover image. (*Deram*)

Right: With the exception of *Wind & Wuthering, Selling England by the Pound* was Genesis' only non-gatefold sleeve of the 1970s. (*Charisma*)

GENESIS

SELLING ENGLAND BY THE POUND

Left: Artist H.R. Giger designed the sleeve and the ELP logo for *Brain Salad Surgery* which hinted at his work for the sci-fi horror classic *Alien* six years later. (*Manticore*)

Right: Helmut Wenske's beautiful artwork for *Remember the Future* was one of several he provided for Nektar in the 1970s. (*Bellaphon*)

Left: In addition to its biblical connotations, the title *On the Third Day* is indicative that this is the Electric Light Orchestra's third album. (*Warner Bros.*)

Right: Although *Solar Fire* is not the adaptation of Gustav Holst's *The Planets Suite* that Manfred Mann had planned, musically, it's far from a compromise. (*Bronze*)

Above: Manfred Mann wearing the familiar hat and glasses, framed by the Earth Band.

Below: Electric Light Orchestra performing 'Showdown' on BBC TV's *Top of the Pops* in October 1973.

Above: During photo sessions, it was almost obligatory for the band members to wear the iconic Magma symbol.

Right: All smiles, there's no indication of the rift that would divide the classic line-up of Yes following the recording of *Tales From Topographic Oceans.*

MÉKANÏK DÉSTRUKTÏW KÖMMANDÖH

MAGMA

.M.D.K.

Left: *Mekanïk Destruktïẁ Kommandöh is* Magma's best-known album and the one that arguably launched the Zeuhl cult. (*A&M*)

Right: Like several album sleeves from the period, only by opening out the gatefold can the full splendour of Roger Dean's artwork for *Tales From Topographic Oceans* be appreciated. (*Atlantic*)

cool, double-tracked sax and piano interplay. It has a distinct Average White Band feel in the vein of their hit 'Pick Up the Pieces' released the following year with glissando guitar adding a layer of spacey-nous.

At 5:40, a persistent vocal line insists we 'Have a cup of tea, have another one' stretched out over an extended, spacey jam where Allen and co do perhaps fall prey to self-indulgence. At 9:11, it's brought back down to earth by powerful, ascending guitar, piano chords and a false ending. It begins anew with more strange voices and sound effects, followed by a drums and percussion sequence with all manner of thumping, clanging and tinkling. A bass, piano and pounding, rat-a-tat drum crescendo brings the track and side one to a noisy but satisfying close.

Side two
'The Pot Head Pixies' 2:59 (Allen)
No sooner has the stylus needle dropped onto side two, and the Pot Head Pixies have landed. They are escorted by a funky combination of drums, bass, rhythm guitar and sax. The male lead vocal is very loose, while the female punctuations – repeating the single word 'crazy' – are a throwback to the psychedelic era of the 1960s. The brief but splendid middle-eight is a quirky merry-go-round ride in 3/4 waltz time with a different male vocal. A return to the main vocal melody is led by sax all the way and that 'crazy' hook would have Austin Powers drooling down his Y-fronts. A climatic sax riff climbs the scales to bring this offbeat offering to a close.

'The Octave Doctors and the Crystal Machine' 1:54 (Tim Blake)
A short, instrumental diversion composed and performed by synth wizard Tim Blake (AKA Hi T Moonweed the favourite). His instrument of choice sounds like an EMS VCS 3, but I could be wrong. It does have a *The Dark Side of the Moon* tone with ambient, new-agey electronic washes. A tone poem of sorts and definitely one for the headphones.

'Zero The Hero and the Witch's Spell' 9:37 (Allen, Blake, Christian Tritsch)
Another lengthy outing, this track has a hesitant intro of percussion, flute and tick-tock rhythm. Glissando chords gatecrash at 0:29, joined by a walking rhythm with flute embellishments and a superbly powerful vocal. At 1:45, a lengthy instrumental bridge features a bongo-style rhythm maintaining a steady beat. A scat vocal segment plays host to a sultry tenor sax solo and rhythm guitar chords. There is another quick burst of vocals before subsiding into another lengthy interlude of haunting effects and a low key but effective guitar pulse.

The mood is broken by a throbbing bassline and at 6:23, it breaks into a stately jog, overlaid by improvised sax soloing, crashing cymbals and stuttering drums. Unchecked, it falls into cacophonic disarray, reaching a peak before subsiding at 8:20. With just the sax motif – and a touch of keyboards – left standing, it develops into a memorable solo before accelerating with funk guitar and a heavy rhythm that races headlong to a breathless conclusion.

'Witch's Song / I Am Your Pussy' 5:10 (Gilli Smyth, Allen)

The concluding track opens with a twangy guitar volley that has more than a touch of Hendrix about it. It's quickly joined by a jaunty sax theme doubled by guitar. The lively, cheek-puffing sax trills are reminiscent of the popular sound that UK band Madness would develop in the early 1980s. As the titular character (The Good Witch Yoni), Gilli Smyth's sensual whispered vocals seem right at home, as does the manic laugh.

The instrumental bridge features yet another sax solo – Didier Malherbe is all over this album – before Allen's distinct accent is evident in the half-spoken / half-sung interlude, replete with wah-wah guitar embellishments. Whispered vocals return, along with the unison sax and bass riff. The mellow female spoken bridge at 3:15 is downright sensuous, again concluding with a manic, electronically treated cackle. The album concludes as bizarrely as it began with an upbeat male singer proclaiming 'I only wanna know yuh' in an almost mock-cockney accent.

Le Orme – *Felona E Sorona*

Personnel:
Toni Pagliuca: keyboards
Aldo Tagliapietra: voice, bass, guitar
Michi Dei Rossi: drums, percussion
Produced at Fonoroma Studios, Milano by Gian Piero Reverberi
Recording date: Completed 20 February 1973
Release date: 1973
Record label: Philips
Highest chart places: UK: Did not chart, USA: Did not chart, Italy: 1
Running time: 32:49

In 1973, the UK boasted symphonic trio Yes, Genesis and ELP, but Italy had its own claim to 'Rock Progressivo Italiano' fame in Premiata Forneria Marconi, Banco del Mutuo Soccorso and Le Orme. While the first two would soon abbreviate their names to a more user-friendly PFM and Banco, respectively, Le Orme – which translates into English as 'The Footsteps' – is memorably succinct in any language. The band's earliest recordings date back to 1967, when they were part of the psychedelic pop scene. With subsequent releases, they evolved into a talented progressive trio, although they were victims of the usual line-up changes.

Felona E Sorona was Le Orme's fourth studio release in their native country and it was hugely successful, resulting in their second gold record. Following in the footsteps of PFM, an English version was released later the same year on the Charisma label with new lyrics penned by friend and fan of the band, Peter Hammill. As principal songwriter with Van der Graaf Generator, he was certainly a competent wordsmith, although he was later dismissive of his own lyrics. David Jackson of VdGG recorded additional sax and flute parts, but they were not used. Singer Aldo Tagliapietra confirmed:

I understand why the record company decided against using them. In their opinion Jackson really should have joined the project right from the start in order for his music to blend in naturally with our ideas.

Tagliapietra was evidently more at ease singing in his native language and the Italian version – the one discussed here – is generally regarded to be the band's masterpiece. The English version did, however, bring Le Orme to the attention of a wider audience, resulting in the band's first tour of the UK.

The concept is unusual, even by prog rock standards. It's the story of two imaginary planets – one called Felona and the other Sorona naturally – whose destinies become entwined. Felona's inhabitants live in the sunlight in peace and harmony, while Sorona is a place of darkness and sorrow. As an unexpected result of divine intervention, both planets are destroyed. The songs were first performed in December 1972 when they toured Italy, supporting

67

Peter Hammill, who was intrigued by the music and the concept, leading to his later involvement.

If, for no other reason than the fact that they were a trio with a singing bassist/guitarist and virtuoso keyboardist, Le Orme are often compared with ELP. They certainly share a classical influence, although Le Orme are less prone to bombast and *Felona E Sorona* displays genuine moments of romanticism and sensitivity. Tagliapietra's alto tenor singing is also closer to Jon Anderson than it is to Greg Lake.

Although I've provided the usual track by track description below, each song on the album segues into the next and, like Marillion's *Misplaced Childhood* from twelve years later, that's the way it should be heard to be fully appreciated. For each of the original Italian track titles, I've added the English translation in brackets. In some cases, these are different from the titles on the English version of the album where, for example, 'L'equilibrio' is retitled 'The Maker'.

Italian artist Lanfranco Frigeri is responsible for the paintings on the front and back of the original album sleeve. Felona is represented by a brightly lit and perfectly formed naked female figure, while the emaciated ghostly male figure is Sorona. On the front, they are sharing a moment of intimacy, while on the back, they are facing away into an uncertain future. The inner sleeve includes the lyrics and a synopsis of the story.

In 2011, a 2CD 'Deluxe Edition' was released, which includes both the Italian and English versions. *Felona E / And Sorona* followed in 2016 and features re-recordings of both versions by the then-current line-up, which toured mainland Europe to promote it. Only drummer Michi Dei Rossi remains from the 1973 trio, but the quality of the recording makes it worth seeking out.

Side one
'Sospesi Nell'Incredibile' ('Suspended in the Incredible') 8:43
(Toni Pagliuca, Aldo Tagliapietra)

The story begins with a celebration of the two planets that coexist in a state of universal harmony. Musically, the album begins as it means to carry on with a strident, swirling organ theme underpinned by a precision staccato rhythm with splashing cymbals and hi-hat. At 2:00, it's the musical equivalent of watching the early morning sun rising over the horizon with majestic organ and cymbal rolls. It eases into Aldo Tagliapietra's thoughtful but assured vocal melody on a wave of shimmering organ. As you may have guessed by now, despite his instrumental dexterity, Toni Pagliuca's keyboard of choice is, for the most part, the organ.

At 4:30, we're off on an extended instrumental jam where the ubiquitous organ adopts a shrill tone, backed by an articulate bassline and a busy and ridiculously complex shuffle drum pattern. At 6:19, the organ makes way for synth, which produces some pretty convincing spacey effects, but the track's second half undoubtedly belongs to Michi Dei Rossi. Despite the presence of keyboards and bass, it's virtually one extended drum solo with a suitably explosive barrage to bring things to a dramatic close.

'Felona' 1:59 (Pagliuca, Tagliapietra)

After the grandstanding opening track, 'Felona' provides two minutes of peace and tranquility. Chiming tubular bells are joined by a lilting vocal melody doubled by rhythmic acoustic guitar. It's a lovely and suitably upbeat song for the planet Felona – from the Italian word 'felice' meaning happy – and gives little indication of the tragedy to come. A short but welcome burst of flute brings this all too brief song to a close.

Compare the acoustic guitar here with Jan Akkerman's riff 28 seconds into Focus' 'House of the King' from two years earlier. They are very similar and both tracks have that same joyful feel.

'La Solitudine Di Chi Protegge Il Mondo' ('The loneliness of those who protect the world') 1:52 (Pagliuca, Tagliapietra)

Another short song, here the supreme being who watches over the worlds – named 'The Maker' on Peter Hammill's English version – reflects on his solitary existence. Suitably, it begins with ethereal voices over rippling waves of sound. The effect is quite mesmerising. The sublime, almost melancholic vocal melody that follows is underpinned by delicate piano arpeggios and haunting keyboard strings. Totally enchanting and the title is almost as long as the track itself.

'L'Equilibrio' ('The Balance') 4:15 (Pagliuca, Tagliapietra)

Following four minutes of respite, the final song on side one is a real tour de force. Although the two planets are unaware of each other, their joint existence provides balance and stability to the universe.

Punctuated by crashing staccato keyboard chords, the vocals launch the song with a nimble bass line, rhythmic organ and shimmering keyboard strings. Organ arpeggios and a touch of Moog enliven the instrumental bridge before classically inspired piano leads a merry dance with shades of Keith Emerson style pomp and flash overlaid with synth flurries. The majestic return to the vocal melody at 3:00 is quite stunning and a real 'hairs standing up on the back of the neck' moment. It's worthy of Yes at their best and closes side one on a high.

Side two
'Sorona' 2:30 (Pagliuca, Tagliapietra)

Side two starts with this tonally sombre song dedicated to the dark planet Sorona – from the word 'sorrow'. Tagliapietra's solemn singing has a church-like hymnal quality, providing a sense of foreboding backed by minimalist keyboard and piano textures.

'Attesa Inerte' ('Inert Waiting') 3:35 (Pagliuca, Tagliapietra)

The mood continues with another brooding vocal, moody bass and hypnotic keys strings. I'm not sure what keyboard Pagliuca uses for the orchestrated arrangements on the album, but it certainly doesn't sound like a Mellotron.

As they gather for their daily ritual to greet the dark, a sudden light in the sky brings new hope to the inhabitants of Sorona. A pulse-like rhythmic loop and vocal round signals a slight upward shift in tempo, which lifts the spirits a little, but even the punchy organ fills fail to break the prevailing mood of melancholia.

'Ritratto Di Un Mattino' ('Portrait of a Morning') 3:25 (Pagliuca, Tagliapietra)

The intro to this song is deceptively tranquil, with eerie keyboard effects joined at 1:20 by haunting harmonised vocals. Felona and Sorona briefly unite, sharing love and happiness which is reflected in the uplifting major key guitar theme at 1:45. It's simply stunning, enhanced by symphonic keys and a stately rhythm that anticipates the melodic style that Camel guitarist Andy Latimer would embrace on later albums like *Music Inspired by The Snow Goose*. It reaches its majestic zenith with a touch of tubular bells before playing out with a minimalist but effective piano solo. Despite some very stiff competition, this is the album highlight, in my view.

'All'infuori Del Tempo' ('Outside of Time') 4:06 (Pagliuca, Tagliapietra)

For the penultimate song, an acoustic guitar rhythm accompanies the delightful pastoral vocal melody with the verses punctuated by organ fills. The keyboard string washes at the halfway mark are a delight and a return to the acoustic-led vocal melody brings with it baroque embellishments. The song really kicks up its heels in the latter part with a martial-like drum pattern before spiralling keyboards and a sweet bass line usher in the symphonic close.

While the people of Sorona rejoice in their newfound happiness, the balance between the two worlds has been disrupted and Felona begins a slow decline into darkness.

'Ritorno Al Nulla' ('Return to Naught') 3:33 (Pagliuca, Tagliapietra)

The final track – an instrumental – is a supreme exercise in controlled power and dynamics. The nihilistic title is an indicator of the sad fate that befalls both Felona and Sorona.

Strident, high-pitched organ chords splashing cymbals and a staccato rhythm pattern provide a dramatic intro and from here on, it doesn't let up. The noodly synth flourishes are very Rick Wakeman with a distinct classical flavour, but this is merely a diversion. It builds powerfully to an intense finale, culminating with a symphonic, and suitably cinematic flourish and the destruction of the two planets.

Jethro Tull – *A Passion Play*

Personnel:
Ian Anderson: lead vocals, flute, acoustic guitar, soprano and sopranino saxophone
Martin Barre: electric guitar
John Evan: backing vocals, piano, organ, synthesizer
Jeffrey Hammond-Hammond: bass guitar, story teller on 'The Story of the Hare
Who Lost His Spectacles'
Barriemore Barlow: drums, percussion, timpani, glockenspiel, marimba
Additional personnel:
David Palmer: orchestra arranger & conductor
Produced at Morgan Studios, London by Ian Anderson & Terry Ellis
Recording date: March 1973
UK release date: 13 July 1973, USA release date: 23 July 1973
Record label: Chrysalis
Highest chart places: UK: 16, USA: 1, Denmark: 4
Running time: 45:05

With the release of the highly acclaimed *Thick as a Brick* in 1972, Jethro Tull had given themselves a tough act to follow. Like Yes' *Close to the Edge* released the same year, it's an acknowledged classic and both albums received unanimous praise from the music scribes. Tull frontman and songwriter Ian Anderson clearly felt he was onto a winning formula and chose another continuous piece of music spread over two sides of vinyl for the follow-up. He could not have anticipated the hostile press reception that awaited his latest concept.

Like Yes' *Tales from Topographic Oceans* released five months later, *A Passion Play* was mauled by American and UK critics alike, especially *Melody Maker* writer and champion of prog-rock Chris Welch. Whereas Yes – with the exception of Rick Wakeman – took the criticism on their collective chins, for Ian Anderson, it was personal. Unlike Jon Anderson and Steve Howe, who were jointly responsible for the concept of *Topographic Oceans*, he was the sole architect of *A Passion Play*.

At the bequest of their management, Tull relocated to the Château d'Hérouville studios in France for the recording of their sixth album. It was an attempt to offset part of their 83% UK tax liability. Recording and living conditions were far from ideal, however, and the sessions were eventually abandoned and the recordings shelved. On the return to London, Anderson elected to begin again with new material. Time was now of the essence and the planned double album was reduced to a single LP. The recording was completed within a single month, although the individual sessions were long and arduous.

The concept is based on Anderson's satirical observations on the afterlife according to Christian faith and the existence of heaven and hell as a representation of good and evil. The plot revolves around one Ronnie Pilgrim who, following his death, attempts to find solace in the afterlife. After experiencing heaven and hell, he ultimately rejects both. None of this is immediately obvious in Anderson's lyrics, which are self-consciously oblique. The album artwork also gives little away. The references to Christian beliefs are evident, however, from the title to the protagonist's name – Pilgrim – to the line in the final verse, 'Roll away the stone from the dark into every-day', which alludes to the resurrection of Christ.

The cover of the gatefold sleeve is a black and white photo of a ballerina lying lifeless on a theatre stage. On the reverse, the ballerina is smiling and dancing against a bright pink background. On the inner spread, a similar pink background is overlaid with two theatre masks representing tragedy and comedy and the lyrics. In the sleeve for the original pressing, tucked inside a curved slot is the faux six-page 'Linwell Theatre' programme. It presents *A Passion Play* as a stage play in four acts – which provide the titles below – but otherwise, it gives no clue as to the narrative. The photos of the imaginary actors are the band members themselves.

Prior to the album's release, the band staged two ambitious shows at London's Empire Pool (now the SSE Arena) on 22 and 23 June 1973, which also failed to impress the critics. Ironically, on 25 August, *Melody Maker* – the same music weekly that damned the shows and the album – ran the headline 'Jethro Retire Hurt!' This was news to Anderson and the other band members and turned out to be a publicity exercise by their manager Terry Ellis.

Although maligned and misunderstood, *A Passion Play* has been reappraised in more recent times and is now recognised as something of a minor classic. Anyone new to the album may wonder what all the fuss was about; it is essentially a cohesive and, for the most part, rewarding listening experience. With LPs averaging 40 minutes, at 45 minutes, it proved to be a long haul for some observers but let's not forget, it is a prog rock album after all. So, pull back the curtains and let the play begin.

Side One
'Act I – Ronnie Pilgrims funeral: a winter's morning in the cemetery' 9:08 (Ian Anderson)

Despite its reputation as a difficult work, *A Passion Play* is blessed with musical themes and hooks that become more appealing with each successive play. The vocal parts do not follow the verse-chorus tradition; instead, they're a stream of consciousness narrative that Anderson wrote very quickly to meet the recording and release deadline. Nonetheless, the recurring lines 'There was a rush along the Fulham Road, into the ever – Passion Play' is a unifying motif throughout.

Act I gets off to an energetic start with stabbing staccato chords followed by a galloping organ riff. With its baroque inversions, it's a medieval musical romp. Clearly, Tull have not lost sight of their folky roots. An abrupt change of mood and tempo leads into the mellow song 'The Silver Cord'. Ronnie Pilgrim has died tragically and as a ghost, he attends his own funeral, where he cries out to his friends, 'Do you still see me even here?' Vocally Anderson has rarely sounded better with discrete backing from piano and acoustic guitar.

A saxophone led jam follows with lively organ and the fast but extremely tight rhythm partnership of Jeffrey Hammond and Barriemore Barlow. Although he had difficulty mastering the instrument, Anderson's soprano sax playing is accomplished throughout and features more prominently than his customary flute. As a result, it found little favour with the other band members. Elsewhere, the music is brimming with superb performances, although Martin Barre's guitar parts are a little subdued at times.

A return to the song section followed by a tranquil acoustic interlude brings Act I to a close.

'Act II – The Memory Bank: a small but comfortable theatre with a cinema screen – the next morning' 14:01 (Anderson)

Act II and *A Passion Play* really gets into its uptempo stride. Anderson's vocal melody trades blows with a complex, stop-start instrumental pattern. A sax-led instrumental section with a great riff is followed by a jazzy flute workout that's more improvised than composed. A hard-rocking song section with bluesy guitar breaks harks back to Tull's formative years. The tricky time signatures and instrumental stops and starts are very Gentle Giant, however.

In the 'Memory Bank', Ronnie Pilgrim's past life is scrutinised by a questioning jury to determine if he is worthy of a place in heaven. An ascending chord progression accelerates like a speeding train before applying the brakes for a mid-tempo vocal section replete with organ stabs.

After more instrumental shenanigans with sudden tempo and key changes with vibrant organ, guitar and sax to the fore, it suddenly grinds to a halt at the 20-minute mark. A brief and mellow reprise of Anderson's now-familiar vocal melody confirms that our protagonist has been granted a place in heaven with a posh English voice proclaiming, 'We won't cross you out'. Finally, a rhythm loop leads the song at a merry dance to the end of part one.

'The Story of the Hare Who Lost His Spectacles' 1:30 (Jeffrey Hammond-Hammond, John Evan, Anderson)

At the halfway mark, this is a whimsical interlude that has no connection with Anderson's concept, either musically or lyrically. A playful diversion, I suspect it was included to demonstrate that Tull were not taking themselves too seriously. Instead, it perplexed reviewers who found its inclusion baffling and unnecessary.

In a comical Monty Python style voice, John Evan announces 'This is The Story of the Hare Who Lost His Spectacles' leaving Jeffrey Hammond to tell the story. It's very much in the style of a children's fable and if I'm not mistaken, A.A. Milne's Winnie the Pooh stories are an obvious influence. It has similar animal characters, including an owl, a kangaroo, a hare – rather than a rabbit – and a bee. Only a bear with an insatiable appetite for honey is missing. The story is interrupted by the record player stylus reaching the end of side one.

Side Two
'The Story of the Hare Who Lost His Spectacles' 2:48
(Hammond-Hammond, Evan, Anderson)

To a light-hearted backing of tuned percussion, piano and orchestrations, Hammond continues his tale on side two. Throughout, he adopts a mock north of England accent that straddles the border between Lancashire and Yorkshire. It's a far cry from Anderson's folky quaver and lyrical references to London and the southeast of England elsewhere on the album. Like all the best children's stories, he breaks into a little song at the end, just as Pooh was prone to do during one of his adventures.

A film version of 'The Story of the Hare Who Lost His Spectacles' was shown as part of the elaborate stage shows on the *A Passion Play* tour.

'Act III – The business office of G. Oddie and Son – two days later' 9:30 (Anderson)

A Passion Play begins where it left off on side one with a reprise of the 'Forest Dance' instrumental which gathers speed, faster and faster before synth punctuations bring it to a dead stop. Anderson croons the mellow 'The Foot of Our Stairs' medieval flavoured melody with acoustic guitar and a punchy rhythm backing. Heaven is not quite what Pilgrim expected and, disappointed, he decides that life – or rather death – would be better down under.

A lengthy, jazz-inflected sax solo develops with organ and guitar providing heavy but fluid support. Another mellow song finds Pilgrim at the offices of G. Oddie and Son, where he's granted a change of venue to hell. As an aside, the comedy series *The Goodies* starring Bill Oddie was hugely popular on UK TV at the time.

A buoyant, circular synth rhythm brings to mind the vintage electronic *Dr Who* TV theme, although it does perhaps overstay its welcome a little. Joined by lively, semi-improvised sax playing, Anderson's vocal finds Pilgrim at odds with Lucifer the moment he arrives in hell.

'Act IV – Magus Perdé's drawing room at midnight' 9:40
(Anderson)

A blast of organ and synth introduces a mid-tempo vocal melody with a sprightly rhythm. Sax, guitar and flute exchange solos while Pilgrim is at the railway station making good his escape from hell. A brief respite comes in the shape of a lilting tune with double-tracked acoustic guitars playing both the rhythm and the melodic hook. This soon gives way to Barre's abrasive lead guitar fills, flute and Hammond's prominent bass line. Anderson's strident vocal finds Pilgrim in the presence of Magus Perdé, who sympathises with his situation.

More tempo and rhythmic chops and changes follow with the combined forces of synth, sax, acoustic guitar, rhythm guitar and vocal leading a merry gallop towards the finish line. With the rejoicing lines 'Living BE!, Here am I!' – Pilgrim is reborn. A final reprise of 'There was a rush along the Fulham Road, into the ever – Passion Play' brings the story and the album to a circular close.

Can – *Future Days*

Personnel:
Holger Czukay: bass, double bass
Michael Karoli: guitar, violin
Jaki Liebezeit: drums, percussion
Irmin Schmidt: keyboards, synthesizers
Kenji 'Damo' Suzuki: vocals, percussion
Produced at InnerSpace Studio, Weilerswist near Cologne by Can
Recording date: 1973
Release date: August 1973
Record label: United Artists
Highest chart places: UK: Did not chart, USA: Did not chart, Germany: Did not chart
Running time: 40:56

One of the leading exponents of Krautrock, Can were not only on the fringes of the prog rock mainstream, but they were virtually off the map. Nonetheless, as far as their influence on successive generations of musicians is concerned, they were the equal of Yes, Genesis, Pink Floyd et al. David Bowie was an admirer and Radiohead's experimentations in electronica owes a good deal to Can's pioneering music. They embraced avant-garde, modern classical, freeform jazz and ambient and two of the key members – Holger Czukay and Irmin Schmidt – studied under famed composer Karlheinz Stockhausen who also hailed from Cologne. Modern jazz pioneer Miles Davis was also a notable influence on Can.

Around the time of *Future Days*, Can made several forays onto British soil and it was during such tours and those by other German bands that the UK press coined the phrase 'Krautrock'. Some bands took offence, which is understandable given their unfamiliarity with the British sense of humour, where irony is often mistaken for sarcasm. Can took it in their stride and gained many fans and enjoyed healthy record sales in the UK, more so than in Germany. When interviewed for *Prog Rock* magazine, Holger Czukay later said, 'We were more or less naturalised into England'.

Formed in Cologne in 1968, *Future Days* was Can's fourth album, not counting the 1970 compilation *Soundtracks*. The line-up responsible had been in existence since 1970, following the departure of American singer Malcolm Mooney. The two previous albums *Tago Mago* (1971) and *Ege Bamyası* (1972) were equally pioneering, inspiring singers and musicians in the UK and America especially. The latter closed with the unlikely hit single 'Spoon', which charted at number 6 in Germany. It wasn't until 1976 and the infectious 'I Want More' that they had their first chart success in the UK, reaching number 26 on 28 August. The title song 'Future Days' featured on the 1997 remix album *Sacrilege,* which was another chart entry in the UK.

Although Can's style and playing are a million miles from the rock mainstream, they were skilled musicians following their natural instincts and musical training. Like many bands before and since, Czukay believes that Can

excelled on stage, more so than in the studio. Even so, as an introduction
to the band, *Future Days* is as good a place as any to start being one of their
most accessible offerings. Singer Damo Suzuki has a unique talent and when
he departed following the recording to become a Jehovah's Witness, it was a
huge loss to the band. Czukay confirmed, 'We tried out many other singers, but
nobody suited us anymore. An era came to an end'.

Much like the music itself, the album cover is a stark, minimalist design with the
band name in bold gold lettering against a dark blue background. The Psi letter
from the Greek alphabet and album title are underneath in a stylised gold frame.
The graphic style was popular at the time and adapted for several album covers.
The reverse is almost identical, with images of the band members replacing the
album title. Although correctly titled on the sleeve, on the original UK pressing,
the side-long track 'Bel Air' is listed as 'Spare a Light' on the LP label.

Side one
'Future Days' 9:34 (Holger Czukay, Michael Karoli, Jaki Liebezeit,
Irmin Schmidt, Damo Suzuki)
The title song opens with the sampled sound of rippling water and electronic
drones and washes – Pink Floyd had nothing on these guys. Slowly, Jaki
Liebezeit's shuffle beat emerges, accompanied by Holger Czukay's single bass
note repeated at every second bar. Distorted sample voices are followed by
a touch of violin that's undeniably haunting but also disorientating to the
untutored ear.

Damo Suzuki's vocals appear discreetly in the background around the four-
minute mark and it's obvious that he is no ordinary singer. His voice, like the
instruments, is used to weave abstract textures and polyrhythms where the
emphasis is on atmosphere rather than melody and no one person dominates.
The hypnotic percussive groove is maintained throughout, with Michael
Karoli contributing mellow, bluesy guitar licks. Without overpowering, the
music gradually builds in intensity with the layering of guitar, voices and Irmin
Schmidt's rhythmic keys before slowly fading almost as discreetly as it began.

Suzuki's lyrics are almost as unorthodox as his vocal style; an improvised
stream of consciousness where each line evolves naturally from the one before:
'With all that breaking home, Was breaking that break up home, Was rolling up,
break the wall, And the tall wind did break your home, roll, roll on'. Although
his first language is Japanese, he spent several years in mainland Europe before
joining Can. Despite his command of English, he had no interest in following
the familiar narrative rules of songwriting. As the song fades, the final line 'For
the sake of future days' is repeated no less than seventeen times.

'Spray' 8:28 (Czukay, Karoli, Liebezeit, Schmidt, Suzuki)
'Spray' continues the band's penchant for short, succinct song titles that
began on the *Tago Mago* album. Like the opening track, this is an atmospheric,

percussive song, although it has more of an improvised feel about it with shades of avant-garde jazz as well as Stockhausen. As is typical of Can's work from this period, they don't follow the conventional rules of popular music. The freeform structure forgoes obvious formalities such as verses, chorus and an instrumental bridge.

At around the six-minute mark, there is the semblance of a melody, although the vocals are again low in the mix before another slow fade. The words are typically elusive, although clearly, Suzuki's first-person protagonist is in a confused state of mind: 'Just don't know where am I, just don't know where I'm going'. I think we've all been in that situation at some point in our lives.

'Spray' is typical of Can's spontaneous and unified approach to constructing their material.

In recognition of the band's influence, both Czukay and Liebezeit would later become in-demand musicians for the art house and new wave set, working with the likes of Brian Eno, Jah Wobble, David Sylvian, Eurythmics and Depeche Mode. Both long-serving members, Karoli took part in reincarnations of Can in the 1980s and 1990s while Schmidt turned his talents to film soundtrack commissions in his native Germany.

'Moonshake' 3:02 (Czukay, Karoli, Liebezeit, Schmidt, Suzuki)

Liebezeit's metronomic, unfaltering beat – which could easily be mistaken for a drum machine – provides the heartbeat for the album's most immediate offering. At a radio-friendly three minutes, 'Moonshake' was released as a single in October 1973 with 'Splash' as the B side, but it failed to emulate the success of 'Spoon' from two years earlier.

It certainly had the potential with a throbbing bass line and chugging guitar riff creating a cool jazz vibe. Suzuki's vocals snake seductively around the incessant rhythm, with keys providing a convincing sax sound. Despite the bizarre electronic squeaks and squawks in the instrumental bridge, it's catchy with an incessant groove that had the power to entice all but the most cautious onto the dance floor.

Can's influence was far-reaching in later decades, leaving its mark on new wave, electropop, synth pop and post rock. In the 1990s, British experimentalists Moonshake were sufficiently inspired by this song to adopt the title as their moniker.

Side two
'Bel Air' 19:53 (Czukay, Karoli, Liebezeit, Schmidt, Suzuki)

This is Can's longest song since 'Yoo Doo Right' on the debut album *Monster Movie* (August 1969), which similarly occupied side two. In four distinct but equally memorable sections, 'Bel Air' features a low key intro with just a hint of a melody. The track bubbles into life as Karoli's left hand darts up and down the fretboard for the open chords with a hint of Mellotron strings from Schmidt drifting in and out in the background. Driven by a light percussive backing, the tempo begins to pick up before dissolving at 4:20.

A funky bass and drum shuffle takes up the mantle with cymbal splashes and a hurried pace that almost develops into a martial rhythm. This is free form jazz at its best, with keys emulating a busy flute tone. A double-time shuffle develops before fading around the nine-minute mark to make way for the next sequence.

The third part builds slowly with Karoli's tastefully sparse jazzy guitar lines and Suzuki's chant-like singing. An eerie guitar phrase comes creeping in from the left channel and, coupled with Liebezeit's dextrous snare and cymbals, we've suddenly strayed into King Crimson territory. At the fifteen-minute mark, things really begin to heat up, building to a peak before release comes in the form of an improvised finale. As each band member gradually bows out, a brief reprise of the opening guitar and percussion statement brings 'Bel Air' full circle.

Despite the twenty-minute playing time, Suzuki is typically economical with his words with variations of the line 'Spinning down alone' and later, 'Breaking down, you know' repeated multiple times. On stage, 'Bel air' was a popular number and would often vary in length depending upon the whims of the band on any given night.

Kayak – *See See the Sun*

Personnel:
Max Werlerofzoiets: lead vocals, percussion, Mellotron
Johan Slager: guitars, backing vocals
Ton Scherpenzeel: keyboards, backing vocals
Cees van Leeuwen: bass, backing vocals, harmonica
Pim Koopman: drums, backing vocals, synthesizer, marimba, lead vocals on 'Lovely Luna' and 'Forever Is a Lonely Thought'
Additional personnel:
Giny Busch: violin on 'Lyrics'
Martin Koeman: violin on 'Lyrics'
Ernst Reijseger: cello on 'Lyrics'
Gerrit-Jan Leenders: vocals, percussion on 'Hope for a Life'
Rijn Peter de Klerk: percussion on 'Hope for a Life'
Gijsbert Perlee: barrel organ 'Flamingo' on 'Mammoth'
Produced at Bovema EMI Studios, Heemstede, The Netherlands by Gerrit-Jan Leenders and Kayak
Recording date: October 1972 to June 1973
Release date: 1973
Record label: The Netherlands: EMI, UK: Harvest
Highest chart places: UK: Did not chart, USA: Did not chart, The Netherlands: Did not chart
Running time: 47:50

While Focus were making waves in the UK and USA in 1973, fellow Dutch band Kayak were enjoying moderate success at home. The debut LP *See See the Sun* was their only album of the 1970s not to enter the Dutch chart, but it did contain two hit singles – 'Lyrics' and 'Mammoth'. It established their reputation as a band that juxtaposed commercial sensibilities with prog rock credibility, which they would pursue with varying degrees of artistic success.

Kayak evolved from the band High Tide Formation in 1972 who started out as Balderdash in 1967. The founding members included Ton Scherpenzeel on piano and bass and Pim Koopman on percussion and guitar. With the change of name to Kayak, Johan Slager was recruited as guitarist, followed by Max Werner on vocals and later Cees van Leeuwen who replaced Jean Michel Marion on bass.

Scherpenzeel and Koopman were now established as the keyboardist and drummer, respectively and wrote the majority of the material for *See See the Sun*, which set the pattern for subsequent releases. The first songs to be recorded were the debut single 'Lyrics' along with the B-side 'Still Try to Write a Book' and 'Mouldy Wood' in October 1972. The majority of the recording, however, took place in May and June 1973 with co-producer Gerrit-Jan Leenders who was also jointly responsible for the arrangements.

Although the songs were recorded in Heemstede, the majority – with the exception of 'Lyrics' and 'Mammoth' – were remixed by recording engineer

Pierre Geoffrey Chateau at Abbey Road Studios in London. He was assisted by Alan Parsons, who engineered *The Dark Side of the Moon* at the same studio a few months earlier. Dave Grinsted – whose engineering credits include Caravan, Gryphon and Focus – remixed 'Lyrics' at Chipping Norton Recording Studios in Oxfordshire. As a result of all this tinkering, *See See the Sun* benefits from a polished sound, particularly for a debut from a relatively unknown band.

Although there are nine songs averaging a little over five minutes in length, *See See the Sun* is a musically ambitious offering where, despite their commercial leanings, Kayak's prog rock credentials are evident. British symphonic rock – and Yes and Gentle Giant in particular – are conspicuous role models, but the band succeed on their own terms thanks to memorable melodies and fine performances, particularly from Ton Scherpenzeel. Kayak lasted for ten years and nine albums but reformed in 1991 and continue under the leadership of Scherpenzeel to this day.

The European and UK album cover designed by Herman Willem Baas is an image of the final 'diamond ring' phase of the total solar eclipse taken in June 1973 by Carel Koppeijzer. The North American release featured a less inspired photo of the band. The rear sleeve shows the band members gazing at the sun through protective eye filters. On the cover, the familiar Kayak logo makes its debut appearance where the last letter 'K' is reversed to emphasise the palindrome symmetry of the band's name.

Side one
'Reason for it All' 6:29 (Ton Scherpenzeel)
The album begins in fine style with a flourish of classical baroque piano. In his teens, Ton Scherpenzeel studied double bass and piano at the Muzieklyceum in Hilversum. Organ and insistent guitar chords lead the band into a memorable vocal melody where the harmonised singing is very early Yes, especially Max Werner's high tenor lead. Although he's credited as Werlerofzoiets on the album sleeve, he changed his name to Werner soon after. Scherpenzeel's first-person lyrics are succinct; he's searching for a meaning to his life and seems to have found the answer in love.

The lengthy instrumental bridge boasts impressive harpsichord soloing while Pim Koopman and Cees van Leeuwen maintain a rock-steady platform for Scherpenzeel's virtuoso flights. At the halfway mark, Johan Slager intervenes with a bluesy, mostly improvised fuzzed guitar solo before an ascending rhythm that comes to a dead stop at 5:21. For the final minute, the lively vocal melody is reprised, driven by synth and guitar.

'Reason for it All' proved to be a popular stage song and remained in the band's repertoire following their reformation and into the current millennium.

'Lyrics' 3:42 (Scherpenzeel)
Koopman introduces the band's first single with a brief but dramatic timpani roll. Scherpenzeel's infectious piano theme is taken over by Werner's harmonious

singing, where the verses and chorus are almost indistinguishable. As the title suggests, this is a song about the difficulty of writing songs where Scherpenzeel takes a pragmatic view – 'If you don't enjoy it, I'm sorry, but it's not meant for you'. Although he was the lead singer, Werner's only song recorded by Kayak was 'Golddust' on the fifth album *Starlight Dancer* released in 1977.

The song has a very proggy midsection thanks to a sprightly, Wakeman flavoured keys solo. The ethereal cat cry sounds in the background should be a distraction but somehow work within the context of the song. It's no wonder that 'Lyrics' reached number 19 in the Dutch top 100 chart when it was released as a single in April 1973 ahead of the album. The B-side 'Try to Write a Book' written by Koopman was a bonus track on the 1995 CD reissue of *See See the Sun*.

'Mouldy Wood' 5:16 (Johan Slager, Pim Koopman, Scherpenzeel)

The third song motors along at a brisk pace with a tricky rhythm and with van Leeuwen's rumbling bass to the fore. Werner is again backed by full band harmonies which are processed during the middle-eight. Although Scherpenzeel shares the musical input to this song, he is once again responsible for the lyrics, which typically are written in the first person. Here, his protagonist is a seaman on a sinking ship of 'mouldy wood' desperate to be rescued: 'Save our souls, save the lives of our people'.

Echoing the fate of the ship's crew, the instrumental break features celestial organ and piano. Slager's spiky guitar lines are pure Gentle Giant, which he exchanges for a melodious cadenza to bring the song – if not the ship – home.

'Lovely Luna' 8:19 (Koopman)

In addition to writing this song, Koopman provides the lead vocals and, despite it being the album's longest offering, his lyrics are minimal. The song's subject is the emotional and disorientating effects attributed to moon sickness with abstract lines like 'Liquid fish and sea is shining bright' bringing to mind Pete Sinfield's expressionistic wordplay.

The song is centred around a monumental – kudos here to producer Gerrit-Jan Leenders – fuzzed guitar riff that could have been lifted from a 1960s Spaghetti Western. The wordless harmonies are heavenly, as are the stirring Mellotron strings. This section is bookended by a haunting song with rippling twelve-string guitar, electric piano and Koopman's vulnerable, precisely phrased singing that has an alluring quality, not unlike Gentle Giant's Kerry Minnear.

Following the appropriately titled fourth album, *The Last Encore*, Koopman left Kayak in 1976 but returned three years later.

Side two
'Hope for a Life' 6:49 (Koopman, Scherpenzeel)

To open side two, we are once again in Gentle Giant territory. Although the melody is slight, the playing is anything but with guitar and bass interlocking superbly while organ, drums and tuned percussion provide the rhythmic foundation. The vocals are delivered in a Yes-like chant fashion, while the unmistakable, earthy growl of van Leeuwen's Rickenbacker 4001 immediately brings Chris Squire to mind.

Scherpenzeel provides just eight lines of verse in which the simple message is that hope is what keeps us alive, even though it's sometimes 'hard to be straight and sincere'. The wordless vocal round that appears at five minutes and again at six minutes into the song is a tip of the hat to a similar sequence in Yes' 'Siberian Khatru' before the band's instrumental might builds to a rousing crescendo.

'Ballet of the Cripple' 4:39 (Cees Van Leeuwen, Koopman, Scherpenzeel)

Van Leeuwen's bass is once again prominent during this mid-tempo song, as are the familiar Yes inspired harmonies with a dash of The Beach Boys. It was the B-side to the band's second single 'Mammoth' and with a basic 4/4 riff and a memorable vocal melody, it has its own radio-friendly appeal. The instrumental bridge featuring organ is suitably uplifting and I particularly like the hushed vocal sequence for the final verse.

The song's uplifting tenor gives little indication of the words which Scherpenzeel co-wrote with van Leeuwen. If my interpretation is correct, it's a scathing indictment of the entertainment industry and how the audience is easily duped, which still rings true today. Interestingly, after he left Kayak in 1975, van Leeuwen became a lawyer specialising in entertainment law before turning his attention to politics.

'Forever is a Lonely Thought' 5:26 (Koopman, Scherpenzeel)

The unaccompanied intro features Slager plucking his acoustic guitar strings in the style of a harp, which also acts as a metronomic, clock-like rhythm for the verses. In addition to writing the music, Koopman once again provides the restrained lead vocal, which gives the song a dreamlike quality. At the two-and-half minute mark, his snare roll brings the song to life with busy drumming and majestic strings adding an epic sweep.

It was Werner rather than Scherpenzeel who played the often temperamental Mellotron 400, although the latter is clearly responsible for the dexterous, jazzy piano solo. Scherpenzeel also wrote the lyrics, which appears to be another personal observation on the difficulty of writing meaningful songs, evident in the chorus 'What does it take, to sell a pretty song'. Common themes that link his songs are insecurity and being in search of something.

'Mammoth' 2:57 (Koopman, Scherpenzeel)

With a jaunty piano and bass theme, this is a radio-friendly song with barrel organ and scratch guitar fills enhancing the carnival atmosphere. There's an obvious Beatles influence and in the lyrics, the despondent protagonist is equating himself to the extinct mammal of the title, which, like the subject of 'I am the Walrus', was renowned for its long tusks. In keeping with the mood, Werner adopts a tongue-in-cheek vocal style, contrasting with the lush harmonies in the bridge.

The second single from the album, 'Mammoth' peaked at number 17 in the Dutch top 100 in August 1973. It was originally recorded without a barrel organ and was twice as long, but the band preferred this version. The bulky instrument – played by guest Gijsbert Perlee from Amsterdam – wouldn't fit in the studio and had to be recorded outside.

'See See the Sun' 4:13 (Van Leeuwen, Koopman, Scherpenzeel)
The title song is a fitting closer with Werner's vocals bringing to mind the dulcet tones of Colin Blunstone, drifting on a sea of piano and organ. His singing here is softer, closer to Koopman's and as a result, the English words are more discernible. For the third verse, the song really comes to life with a wonderful vocal hook and Scherpenzeel's accordion providing the delightful instrumental bridge. The counterpoint harmonies are heavenly before ending as it begins with a surge of Mellotron strings.

Van Leeuwen provides the words and, in contrast to 'Ballet of the Cripple', the subject is an edifying celebration of evolution and the natural wonders of the world. The song's intricacies were perhaps lost on radio and, as the third and final single from the album released in December 1973, it failed to trouble the charts. The B-side 'Give it a Name' with Koopman on lead vocals was the second of two CD bonus tracks on the 1995 reissue of *See See the Sun*. In more recent times, Kayak's first four singles, including 'See See the Sun', have been performed live as a medley.

Gentle Giant – *In A Glass House*

Personnel:
Gary Green: six-string electric guitar, twelve-string acoustic guitar, steel guitar, mandolin, tambourine, treble recorder
Kerry Minnear: Moog, Hammond organ, piano, Clavinet, electric piano, Thomas Organ, clavichord, RMI 368 Electra-Piano and harpsichord, celesta, glockenspiel, marimba, vibraphone, tympani, cello, descant recorder, lead vocals
Derek Shulman: lead vocals, alto saxophone, soprano saxophones, descant recorder
Ray Shulman: bass guitar, acoustic guitar, violin, tambourine, backing vocals
John Weathers: drums, bass drum, cowbell
Produced at Advision Studios, London by Gentle Giant & Gary Martin
Recording date: July 1973
Release date: 21 September 1973
Record label: WWA Records
Highest chart places: UK: Did not chart, USA: Did not chart
Running time: 38:08

Gentle Giant may not have been one of the most commercially successful bands of the 1970s, but they were certainly one of the most original and innovative. From early 1970 to the summer of 1980, they released eleven critically acclaimed studio albums and a live double LP. They were renowned for their ambitious vocal arrangements and complex musical structures, embracing rock, folk, madrigal, classical, blues, soul, jazz and avant-garde. Their intense musical chops and changes, and use of minor chords and medieval rhythms presented a challenge to even the most seasoned prog rock fan. Only occasionally, however, did virtuosity take precedence over formal structure and melody.

When Gentle Giant came to record their fifth album, *In A Glass House,* they had two hurdles to overcome. The first was to match the artistic and critical success of its predecessor *Octopus.* The second – and more crucially – was to overcome the loss of founding member Phil Shulman. He, along with his brothers Derek and Ray, formed the band from the ashes of 1960s psychedelic rockers Simon Dupree and the Big Sound.

Fortunately, Gentle Giant were a versatile, multi-talented collective that could turn their hand to a variety of traditional and non-traditional instruments. As a result, Derek was able to cover the saxophone parts that previously would have been played by Phil. Even so, his departure took its toll on the band and the writing and recording of *In A Glass House* proved to be a difficult experience.

On 2 October 1973, shortly after the album's release, I was fortunate enough to see the band during their UK tour. The unlikely venue was the Palais de Dance for Leicester Polytechnic's annual Freshers Ball. Back then, it wasn't uncommon for rock bands to play such events, although the convoluted time signatures of Gentle Giant was hardly the stuff of dance music.

Revisiting this album nearly 50 years on, it's difficult to fathom why Gentle Giant never even came close to the same commercial success enjoyed by acts such as ELP, Genesis and King Crimson. In the liner notes for the CD reissue, Derek Shulman wryly observed, 'In Britain, it's not been low profile, it's been no profile'.

While their music demands a level of commitment from the listener, the same can be said for many of their contemporaries. Paradoxically, the music is also replete with memorable themes and hooks, juxtaposing moments of pastoral elegance with riffs that any hard rock or metal band would be proud of.

Although fame and fortune eluded Gentle Giant in their home country, their star shone brighter in the USA and Canada, where they gigged regularly. Even so, their American record label Columbia refused to release the album whereupon it became a top-selling import, shifting 150,000 copies. Their influence is evident in later generations of US prog bands, including Happy The Man, Echolyn and Spock's Beard. They still command a loyal worldwide following to this day; when the all-encompassing *Unburied Treasure* 30 CD box-set was released in 2019, the initial pressing sold out within a week. Much of the band's classic material has been remixed and reissued on vinyl, CD and Blu-ray in recent years, although unfortunately, the master tapes for *In A Glass House* are presumed lost.

The album cover is a photo negative style collage of the band members. The original LP cover is overlaid with cellophane to create a three-dimensional effect and the UK cover is a mirror image of the German cover on the Vertigo label.

Side one
'The Runaway' 7:15 (Derek Shulman, Ray Shulman, Kerry Minnear)
The sound of breaking glass – sampled from a BBC sound effects record – opens the song and evolves into a lopped rhythm. Organ bubbles to the surface, joined by Gary Green's trebly guitar fills that almost overshadow Derek Shulman's vocals which seem a tad low in the mix. The lengthy instrumental bridge is superb, full of twists and turns with a touch of sweet wordless harmonies and dazzling organ arpeggios. Derek sings in a madrigal style, relating the tale of a man who has broken out of jail and is on the run. His freedom, however, is marred with regret.

Kerry Minnear's marimba solo around the five-minute mark is an unexpected but engaging diversion, while John Weathers' gymnastic 6/8 rhythm was reputedly taken from a Buddy Rich song. Although 'The Runaway' is an excellent opening salvo, given the subject and downbeat one-line chorus – 'And yet his joy is empty and sad' – the mood is almost too uplifting.

Some CD reissues of the album contain as a bonus track a live coupling of 'The Runaway' with 'Experience' recorded in Düsseldorf, Germany, in September 1976. A live version recorded at Palesports in Torino, Italy, in January 1975 is included – along with 'Way of Life' – on the *In A Palesport House* live CD released in 2000.

'An Inmate's Lullaby' 4:40 (D Shulman, R Shulman, Minnear)

In keeping with the 'Lullaby' of the title, this song has a gentle, almost childlike charm. The band were always willing to experiment and here, there isn't a guitar or keyboard in sight. Instead, tuned percussion and the occasional drum beat provide the only backing.

A layering of glockenspiel, marimba and vibraphone – all courtesy of Minnear – provide a delicate backdrop to Derek's processed vocal. The subject here could almost foreshadow the previous song – a patient in a mental institution contemplates his incarceration and state of mind: 'Why does everybody else think that I'm mad'. Minnear is also responsible for the tympani and drum punctuations in the instrumental break and, although these are seemingly random, the arrangement is meticulously crafted.

Minnear is undoubtedly one of the most underrated and gifted musicians of his generation and undeservedly, his keyboard skills never received the same due recognition as many of his contemporaries.

'Way of Life' 7:52 (D Shulman, R Shulman, Minnear)

Following the shout 'Go' – courtesy of Gary Green, 'Way of Life' is out of the starting gate like a thoroughbred with Green's frantic guitar and Ray Shulman's nimble bass line propelling the song at an energetic pace. Organ doubles guitar to perfection with a touch of piano and the central hook is a triumphant call to arms. Minnear's Moog solo is short but most definitely sweet. At 2:30, a baroque interlude featuring church-like organ, violin and Minnear's fragile singing recalls the lyrical 'Think of Me with Kindness' from the previous album *Octopus*. The message here is that everyone must find their own way in life and hopefully, they will come to a mutual understanding with the person they love.

At the halfway mark, the song breaks into its triumphant stride, although it soon takes a more ominous, minor-key turn before guitar, synth and bass return to the main theme. At 5:30, there's a reprise of the regal organ and synth melody and at 6:10, organ returns and slowly fades to bring the track and side one to a calming conclusion.

This is the author's favourite track on the album and one I never tire of hearing – it's prog rock at its finest. In July 1973, Gentle Giant performed 'Way of Life' for a radio session and if anything, the opening section then is taken at an even more frantic pace.

Side two

'Experience' 7:50 (D Shulman, R Shulman, Minnear)

Side two opens with another sonically dense offering. Guitar, Hammond and electric piano lead a merry – if tricky – dance around Minnear's first-person vocals portraying a man reflecting on the folly of his youth. Musically, it has a touch of the avant-garde and Frank Zappa about it, twisting and turning in 9/8 time. Ray works in a solo bass riff that repeats the vocal line, joined by guitar and keys, playing a counterpoint theme to dizzying effect.

Minnear provides a tranquil respite with tuned percussion, organ, clavichord and the band's renowned intricate harmonies taking up the medieval mantle. Only in maturity is the protagonist able to realise how his selfish actions hurt those around him: 'Now I am a man, I realise my unworldly sins pained many lives'. Like many of the band's more subtle moments, it boasts a deceptively clever arrangement.

Green's jagged power chords and Derek's strident vibrato propel the song in a more conventional heavy rock direction, although there's never ever anything conventional about Gentle Giant. Green is allowed a moment of indulgence with a trademark but still inventive, bluesy guitar solo before playing out with the main theme to bring the song full circle.

Often coupled with 'The Runaway', 'Experience' was performed live by the band throughout 1974 and 1975.

'A Reunion' 2:11 (D Shulman, R Shulman, Minnear)

After the drama of the previous song, 'A Reunion' is a pastoral interlude before the album's main event. Minnear once again provides the lead vocal with his usual fragile warmth. It's the story of a chance meeting between two people who were once very close and recalling those once shared, but now long lost, hopes and dreams. It features a beautiful baroque-style string arrangement with Minnear's cello and Ray's lyrical violin weaving its way magically through the song. It's a further demonstration of the band's instrumental dexterity. In their prime, Gentle Giant's dynamic live performances usually involved a rotating combination of over 30 different instruments.

'In a Glass House' 8:26 (D Shulman, R Shulman, Minnear)

Although *In a Glass House* is often cited as a concept album, there is very little evidence given the absence of a narrative thread linking the songs. The 'People who live in glass houses shouldn't throw stones' aphorism doesn't seem to fit either, not even in the title song. The words here are more oblique, but the message seems to be that living in a glass house is a metaphor for having a distorted perspective on life where the glass can also reflect. The chorus – 'Shadow fills the light until the glass house becomes the night, Dark is gleaming or am I dreaming' – suggests the biblical phrase 'Through a glass, darkly', which is much used in literature and has its origins in Corinthians 13:12.

Either way, the band whip up a complex instrumental concoction that moves at a rapid rate, only pausing for Derek's vocal interjections. Weathers gives a tour-de-force performance, holding down the complex rhythm before leading the band in several directions while Ray's bass nails the shuffle groove. With its incessant riff and Derek's strident vocal, there is something very Jethro Tull about this song. During a rare moment of calm, Green's twelve-string acoustic guitar shines a light on the shade and unusually, he throws in a steel guitar solo which adds a distinct country twang to proceedings.

The track and the album appear to fade around the seven and half minute mark, but the band are not quite done. At 7:46, the breaking glass that opened the album is reprised, followed by blink-and-you-miss-it snippets of 'The Runaway', 'Way of Life', 'Experience', 'In A Glass House', 'An Inmate's Lullaby' and 'A Reunion'. A final shattering of glass bounces between the left and right speakers before disappearing into the distance. Now they're done.

Premiata Forneria Marconi – *Photos of Ghosts*

Personnel:

Franco Mussida: vocals, electric and acoustic guitar, twelve-string guitar, theorbo, mandocello

Flavio Premoli: spinet, keyboards, Hammond organ, Minimoog, Mellotron, tubular bells, harpsichord, piano, vocals

Mauro Pagani: flute, piccolo, violin, vocals

Giorgio Piazza: bass guitar, vocals

Franz Di Cioccio: drums, percussion, vocals

Original Italian production at Fonorama Studios, Milan by PFM and Claudo Fabi

Italian recording date: October 1972

Produced at Command Studios, London by Peter Sinfield

UK recording date: February 1973

Release date: October 1973

Record label: Manticore

Highest chart places: UK: Did not chart, USA: 180, Australia: 55

Running time: 39:02

With their fame and fortune growing at a rapid rate, Emerson, Lake & Palmer formed their own record label in 1973. The name – Manticore – was taken from a mythical beast that featured on their 1971 album *Tarkus*. The most significant signing – apart from ELP themselves – was the Italian band Premiata Forneria Marconi in early 1973. Greg Lake witnessed their talents first hand at a launch party in Rome in December 1972 for their second album *Per Un Amico*. Formed in 1970, they were already hugely popular in their home country, but it was the patronage of ELP and Manticore that brought them to the attention of an international market, particularly in the UK and USA. The band's name, taken from a bakery in their home town of Milan where they rehearsed, was also abbreviated to a more user-friendly PFM. Fellow Italian proggers Banco del Mutuo Soccorso later joined Manticore, shortened their name and achieved similar success in America.

A significant factor in PFM's international success was that the four studio albums released under the Manticore banner *Photos of Ghosts* (1973), *The World Became the World* (1974), *Chocolate Kings* (1976) and *Jet Lag* (1977) all featured English lyrics, overcoming the language barrier in North America, Australia and Britain. The man responsible for providing the new lyrics to the first two releases was King Crimson and ELP associate Pete Sinfield who also handled production duties. Sinfield, like Lake, was immediately impressed by the band and, despite the new lyrics, he recognised the importance of allowing the band to retain their Italian musical identity, which had provided the initial attraction.

Their breakthrough album *Photos of Ghosts* was an adaptation of *Per Un Amico* with several modifications. The band travelled to London in January 1973 to begin the recording. Sinfield provided all new words – with the exception of 'Il Banchetto', which remained in Italian – and also added lyrics to 'Mr. 9 'Till 5', originally an instrumental entitled 'Generale'. 'Celebration' – the band's best-known tune – is a re-arranged version of 'È Festa' from the 1972 debut album *Storia Di Un Minuto,* while the instrumental 'Old Rain' was written specifically for the new album. The combination of Sinfield's lush production and the virtuoso quintet of Flavio Premoli, Franco Mussida, Mauro Pagani, Franz Di Cioccio and Giorgio Piazza resulted in a stunning slice of classic prog that ranks amongst the best releases from this era. PFM were not just another emerging prog band; their level of sophistication put them alongside the prog elite, with King Crimson, Yes, Jethro Tull and ELP being conspicuous role models.

PFM's UK concert debut was in Fulham, London, on 24 March 1973 and they played the final day of the Reading Festival on Sunday 26 August. America beckoned and their 1974 tour was the first by an Italian band. In the liner notes for the 2010 CD reissue of *Photos of Ghosts,* drummer Franz Di Cioccio explained: 'Our debut album on an international level meant that every international listener could become aware of a new Italian musical identity that hadn't previously been considered'.

In addition to Sinfield's involvement and a new album title – the original translated into English as *For a Friend* – another distinctive feature of *Photos of Ghosts* is the cover artwork. The pastel colours and pastoral English scene ringed by roses is a far cry from the surreal images that graced the covers of *Storia Di Un Minuto* and *Per Un Amico.*

Side one
'River of Life' ('Appena Un Po')' 6:56 (Flavio Premoli, Franco Mussida, Mauro Pagani, Peter Sinfield)

Photos of Ghosts is a high watermark for PFM and the majestic opening song is arguably their crowning achievement. It boasts a glorious melody, classically inspired arrangement, stunning musicianship and rich harmonies. The symphonic grandeur brings 'And You and I' in particular to mind and like Yes' mini-epic, 'River of Life' plays down the chorus in favour of a sweeping theme for Mellotron, Moog and piano.

Sinfield's lyrics are akin to a geography lesson telling of a river beginning its life underground and meandering its way over waterfalls and past cities to the sea. There's also an ecological message in the line 'Waste and poison cloy where once men drank'. Unfortunately, the words have not dated as well as the music with the opening line 'River of life, rain was your berth' being another awkward example.

As such, the original Italian version 'Appena Un Po' is arguably the stronger of the two. It also features a longer ambient intro, otherwise, it's the same backing. A delicate classical guitar melody is taken up by flute, harpsichord and Hammond before the rhythm section gate crashes the party to propel the arrangement forward. The guitar is mostly restrained, but there is some neat Robert Fripp-inspired fret work from Franco Mussida.

'Celebration' ('È Festa') 3:50 (Premoli, Mussida, Sinfield)

The exuberant, mostly instrumental 'Celebration' received airplay in the UK and North America, but it was a hit single that never was. The original 'È Festa' has the same feel and energy as 'Hocus Pocus' by Focus, released six months earlier, including a touch of Thijs van Leer-style scat singing. Although purists may disagree, 'Celebration' is the more polished version, although 'È Festa' has its charm featuring full-blooded guitar riffing. Either way, only the most cynical soul could not get swept away by the Minimoog's bubbling energy.

In contrast, the middle-eight is very lyrical and the four lines of verse are a celebration of new-found love: 'You've spent a long time waiting, For a perfect yesterday, Now fill your heart with celebration, For that's love's way'. The brief, four-note motif that follows recalls 'The Good, the Bad and the Ugly' theme by fellow Italian Ennio Morricone, although this was no doubt an unconscious inclusion by keyboardist Flavio Premoli.

'Photos of Ghosts' ('Per Un Amico') 5:20 (Premoli, Mussida, Pagani, Sinfield)

Like 'River of Life', the poetic title song is a remixed version of the original with new vocals. More typical of Sinfield's abstract lyrical style, it's a eulogy to the passing of the spirit of youth: 'Of the days we ran and the days we sang'. Despite the reworking, the elaborate arrangements could have only originated from an Italian band. The heavily accented vocals also reveal just how alien English was to the band, although the engaging harmonies easily compensate. Esoteric Recordings' remastered reissue of the album in 2010 features as a bonus track, an 'Instrumental Mix' of 'Photos of Ghosts', which is well worth a listen.

The mood and tempo are more restrained than the previous two tracks, but it does kick up its heels at the halfway mark. A lively gipsy-style violin reel sets the scene for frantic strummed acoustic guitar and rumbling bass. It provides the grounding for a sizzling Minimoog fanfare before a sumptuous piano and synth conclusion brings Genesis – and Tony Banks in particular – to mind.

'Old Rain' 3:40 (Premoli)

The original *Per Un Amico* album has a playing time of under 35 minutes, so the band recorded 'Old Rain' in London in February 1973 to flesh out the English version. This serene instrumental is no mere filler, however, although it does feel like an impromptu take improvised in the studio. That said, Flavio Premoli takes sole writing credit and provides the sparse piano textures. The rest of the band pitch in with classical guitar, delicate cymbal taps, moody bass, lyrical violin and a lovely flute melody.

The title was no doubt inspired by the unwelcoming, mid-winter weather that greeted PFM when they arrived in London in January. 'Old Rain' is not a million miles from one of the more tranquil offerings from 1970s era King Crimson with violinist David Cross, and brings side one to a calming conclusion.

Side two

'Il Banchetto' ('The Banquet') 8:34 (Premoli, Mussida, Pagani)

PFM elected not to re-record the vocals for 'Il Banchetto', which opens side two just as it did on *Per Un Amico*. The band, and Franco Mussida in particular, are clearly more at ease singing in their native tongue and it saved Sinfield the task of penning new words. Ironically, when the band started out in the 1960s under the name I Quelli, their speciality was recording Italian versions of English hit songs.

Translated into English, the title refers to a royal banquet presided over by a King who invites 'The Poet, The Assassin and The Pope'. The King cannot understand why the poor people outside the palace gates are not as happy as he and his guests. In keeping with the song's initial premise, it has a stately grandeur, although the lyrical content is kept to a minimum, allowing the band's instrumental dexterity to shine through. In addition to some lengthy synth excursions, it features tasteful acoustic guitar picking from Mussida and a glorious Keith Emerson style piano solo from Premoli. It's no surprise that 'Il Banchetto' remains a band and fan favourite that is still being performed well into the 21st century.

'Mr. 9 'Till 5' ('Generale') 4:07 (Premoli, Mussida, Sinfield)

This started out as a rousing instrumental entitled 'Generale' – 'General' in English – and although the backing is essentially the same, the lyrics add a whole new perspective. Rechristened 'Mr. 9 'Till 5', it's a mocking observation on the banality of working a daily routine in an office. Although it never occurred to me at the time, even though I worked in an office, Sinfield's words now seem overly patronising. Even more so when the song goes on to suggest that the protagonist's humdrum existence extends outside the workplace.

Thankfully, the music's power and restless energy aren't diminished, although the punctuating keyboard stabs in 'Generale' are reigned in to make way for the vocals. It still sounds like a collision between ELP and Gryphon with jazzy piano flights that once again channel Emerson. As for the angular guitar riff, if you ever wondered where Greg Lake got the idea for the spiky lead break in ELP's *Still...You Turn Me On*, look no further.

Along with 'Celebration', this is one of the album's most enduring songs and both feature on the 1974 live album *Cook*. An instrumental version is a bonus track on the 2010 CD reissue of *Photos of Ghosts*.

'Promenade the Puzzle' ('Geranio') 7:35 (Premoli, Mussida, Pagani, Sinfield)

Following the not altogether successful social commentary of 'Mr. 9 'Till 5', Sinfield retreats to the lyrical style he pioneered with King Crimson for the final song. Surreal lines such as 'Church bells played by a penguin' and 'Fish eat stolen keys in rivers' are capable of confounding even the most perceptive listener.

The meticulously structured arrangement is just as imaginative with playful violin, piano, pipe organ and a waltz-time rhythm conjuring up images of carousels and all the fun of the circus. It's a perfect soundtrack for Sinfield's kaleidoscopic wordplay that echoes 'Cirkus (including Entry of the Chameleons)' that opened Crimson's *Lizard* album in 1970.

Around half a minute shorter than the original 'Geranio' – Italian for 'Geranium' – 'Promenade the Puzzle' negates the slow build that follows the initial verses. The catchy wordless vocal theme remains intact, however, as does the finale of tubular bells and strident synth building to a crescendo before slowly receding into the distance.

Although drummer Franz Di Cioccio and bassist Giorgio Piazza proved to be a successful partnership, the latter was replaced by Patrick Djivas prior to recording the next album, which would display jazz fusion influences. Another popular stage song, 'Promenade the Puzzle,' was resurrected as recently as 2019 during PFM's UK tour.

Renaissance – *Ashes Are Burning*

Personnel:
Annie Haslam: vocals, backing vocals
John Tout: keyboards, backing vocals
Jon Camp: bass, electric and acoustic guitars, vocals, backing vocals
Terence Sullivan: drums, percussion, backing vocals
Additional personnel:
Michael Dunford: acoustic guitar
Andy Powell: electric guitar on 'Ashes Are Burning'
Richard Hewson: string arrangements on 'Can You Understand?' and 'Carpet of the Sun'
Produced at De Lane Lea Studios, Wembley, London by Dick Plant & Renaissance
Recording date: April to August 1973
Release date: October 1973
Record label: Sovereign
Highest chart places: UK: Did not chart, USA: 171
Running time: 40:39

Renaissance mark one was formed in 1969 by ex-Yardbirds Keith Relf and Jim McCarty. They combined folk, jazz, avant-garde and psychedelic rock with the classical piano talents of John Hawken. In 1970, the band fragmented during the recording of the second album *Innocence* and eventually, a completely different and far more enduring line-up was assembled. In addition to the name, they retained the folk and classical elements and forged a melodic style with a similar appeal to that of Genesis, Barclay James Harvest and later, The Enid. Featuring the velvet voice of Annie Haslam, they were also a precursor to 21st-century female-fronted acts like Mostly Autumn, Magenta and Landmarq.

Following the departure of the original line-up, Hawken's colleague from The Nashville Teens, guitarist Michael Dunford assumed leadership of Renaissance. Several intermediate musicians came and went before the line-up of Haslam, keyboardist John Tout, bassist Jon Camp and drummer Terence Sullivan was established in early 1972 for the third album *Prologue*. Guitarist Rob Hendry also played on *Prologue,* but he left following the recording. In the meantime, Dunford remained mostly behind the scenes as principal songwriter, aided by lyrics courtesy of poet and friend of the band Betty Thatcher.

Ashes Are Burning is the fourth studio album to bear the Renaissance name and their most accomplished thus far. I was introduced to the band and the album by the savvy owner of an independent record store in October 1973 while buying the newly released *Selling England by the Pound*. He held up the Renaissance LP and said, 'If you like Genesis, you'll love this', and when he played the opening song 'Can You Understand', I was hooked. It remains my favourite from the band despite later artistic successes, including the acclaimed *Scheherazade and Other Stories* album in 1975.

In addition to Annie Haslam's singing, John Tout's fluid and classically influenced piano playing sets the band apart from their contemporaries, dominating the instrumental set pieces. With the exception of the title song, the absence of electric six-string allows Jon Camp to shine as a lead instrumentalist, in addition to providing a solid rhythm platform with drummer Terence Sullivan.

Like many bands at the time, Renaissance had greater success in America than they did on home soil. On the strength of their breakout single 'Northern Lights', which made it to number 10 in the UK chart in the summer of 1978, the eighth album, *A Song for All Seasons,* was their highest charting in the UK, peaking at 35.

The legendary Hipgnosis are responsible for the cover artwork, although it's not one of their most inspired. The gatefold sleeve features a grainy photo of the band with Haslam and Sullivan on the front and Camp and Tout on the reverse. The now-familiar Renaissance logo is better, making its debut appearance. On the inner sleeve, the bassist is incorrectly named as 'John' Camp.

Side one
'Can You Understand' 9:49 (Michael Dunford, Betty Thatcher)
Some songs are born to open albums and 'Can You Understand' is one such song. The instrumental prelude, in particular, is stunning; a quasi-classical adrenaline rush of ascending piano arpeggios and cascading strings. Dunford is credited with writing the music on all but one of the album's six tracks, but there's a general consensus that John Tout and Jon Camp were responsible for the two-and-a-half-minute intro. Either way, it's the piano and bass – supported by Terence Sullivan's shuffle rhythm and Richard Hewson's string arrangement – that gives the sequence its poise and power.

There's no doubting the authorship of the lyrics; Betty Thatcher was by now a seasoned writer for Renaissance. Her verses are sublime and the chorus typically optimistic: 'Open up your eyes and make the day shine sunshine now' brought to life by Annie Haslam's pitch-perfect soprano.

Renaissance are no strangers to borrowing uncredited orchestral pieces and at 5:25, they incorporate a melody entitled 'Tonya and Yuri Arrive at Varykino' from the 1965 film *Doctor Zhivago*. It's a beautifully performed, one-minute sequence with piano supported by strings, brass and percussion. It wasn't, however, a traditional Russian folk tune as Dunford believed, but the work of composer Maurice – father of Jean-Michel – Jarre who took exception and litigation followed. Jarre composed the music for several of director David Lean's prestigious epics, including *Lawrence of Arabia* and *Doctor Zhivago*, both of which won him Academy Awards for Best Original Score.

To the band's credit, Richard Hewson's majestic, cascading strings transition to the vocal melody at 6:32 is dazzling. A recapitulation of the intro brings the music full circle, providing a spectacular finale.

'Let It Grow' 4:15 (Dunford, Thatcher)

Following the grandiose heights of the opening track, this is a less ambitious but no less engaging song. It opens with a delightful eight-note piano motif before Haslam takes over for the gorgeous vocal melody. Unusually, the verses are more memorable than the chorus, although the singing is perfect throughout, with Haslam hitting impossibly high notes for the words 'slow' and 'flow' in the two-line chorus. She's relating the story of a budding relationship where the message is to slow down and get to know each other, love should not be hurried. Wise words indeed.

The instrumental bridge, featuring Tout's piano arpeggios rising an octave after each repeat, is simple but incredibly effective. At 3:10, in true sonata style, he returns to the intro theme, but the arrangement is now richer, embellished by Sullivan's meticulous drumming and the whole band led by Haslam combining for the infectious, wordless choral hook.

'On the Frontier' 4:53 (Jim McCarty, Thatcher)

When Jim McCarty formed Renaissance at the beginning of 1969, he had an uphill task trying to shake off his blues-rock associations with the Yardbirds. This was despite the excellent self-titled debut album released in October that year. Although the original line-up had dissolved by the following summer, McCarty remained in contact with Renaissance, providing the occasional song. He had already recorded a version of 'On the Frontier' earlier in 1973 with his short-lived band Shoot and it was the title song of their only album.

Camp has a greater presence on this song which has a sunny, folk-pop vibe. His chugging acoustic guitar opens proceedings and he shares singing duties with Haslam, with his voice the more prominent. The 'frontier' of the title and chorus is a metaphor for standing on the cusp of a new day, bringing with it fresh hope and expectations.

Although the vocal melody is more than decent and the harmonies superb, again, it's the instrumental sections that really scratch the listener's progressive rock itch. Around the two minute mark, synth introduces a short, but uplifting theme, followed by Beethoven inspired piano and bass exchanges. The piano coda brings the song and side two to a graceful conclusion.

Side two
'Carpet of the Sun' 3:31 (Dunford, Thatcher)

Similar to 'On the Frontier', this has a relaxed, upbeat feel, although here, the acoustic guitar and harpsichord are sugar-coated by Hewson's lush strings and woodwind arrangement. It's Haslam's soaring delivery that's the focal point; however, flying so high, she almost reaches the stratosphere. The song is a simple, heartfelt celebration of the natural world in which we live: 'Sands upon the shores of time, of oceans mountains deep'.

'Carpet of the Sun' would have made a very fine single and at a radio-friendly three-and-a-half minutes, it must have crossed the band's minds.

Unsurprisingly, it was a popular stage song and along with 'Can You Understand' and 'Ashes are Burning', it features on the excellent double LP *Live at Carnegie Hall* recorded during a three-night residency in New York in June 1975.

Around 1970, Renaissance cut a demo version of 'Carpet of the Sun' with Jane Relf on vocals and John Hawken on piano. The arrangement is very similar to the 1973 version – minus the orchestrations – with an additional verse. Relf's interpretation is stunning, although compared with Haslam, her voice has more of a Joan Baez style folky presence. Hawken's piano is also excellent; he was clearly a role model for Tout's style of playing within the band.

'At the Harbour' 6:50 (Dunford, Thatcher)

The penultimate song features the album's most evocative words. It's a poignant lament for the women waiting in vain for the return of their loved ones who are out fishing in treacherous seas. There's a similar lyric and sentiment in the song 'The Women Were Watching' written by Anthony Phillips and Richard Scott that featured on the ex-Genesis guitarist's 1983 album *Invisible Men*.

Musically, it continues the Renaissance habit of borrowing liberally from the classics; in this case, Claude Debussy's prelude for solo piano 'La Cathédrale Engloutie' – 'The Sunken Cathedral' – first published in 1910. It's a striking piece, compellingly performed by Tout and perfectly in tune with the song proper that begins around the two-minute mark. The vocal melody is beautifully conceived, with Haslam singing from the heart to a lyrical backing of classical guitar and harmonium. Five minutes in, 'La Cathédrale Engloutie' is reprised, although Tout's playing is now a little more restrained, allowing Haslam's ethereal choral lament to share the final honours.

'Ashes are Burning' 11:24 (Dunford, Thatcher)

The album is bookended by the two longest tracks, with the title song bringing up the rear. It opens with the sound of wind, delicate cymbal rides and piano before Haslam invites the listener to join her on a journey where there's 'Roads leading everywhere'. Like many of Thatcher's lyrics, the song has a positive outlook on life: the burning embers of the past can signpost the present, so clear your mind and embrace the here and now with its infinite possibilities.

The chorus is catchy, and following Camp's short but prominent Rickenbacker riff, Tout muscles his way through the lengthy instrumental fugue with fast cascading piano notes doubled by harpsichord. He follows through with a moody organ solo which builds to a crescendo before coming to a dead stop at 7:15. Haslam returns for a tranquil reprise of the vocal melody with a sparse backing of organ. When she hits another of those impossibly high notes at 8:35, it's the cue for guest Andy Powell on loan from Wishbone Ash to cut loose with a soaring guitar cadenza, leading the way to the majestic finale, fuelled by Sullivan's explosive drum punctuations.

On stage, 'Ashes are Burning' provided an opportunity for the band to flex their musical muscles and a near 24-minute version occupies the fourth side of the double LP *Live at Carnegie Hall* recorded in 1975 and released the following year. The 2019 remastered reissue of *Ashes Are Burning* features three bonus tracks 'Can You Understand', 'Let It Grow' and 'Ashes Are Burning' recorded on 3 January 1974 at London's Paris Theatre for the BBC Radio One *In Concert* series.

Caravan – *For Girls Who Grow Plump in the Night*

Personnel:
Pye Hastings: electric and acoustic guitars, lead vocals
Peter Geoffrey Richardson: viola
Dave Sinclair: organ, piano, electric piano, Davoli synthesizer
John G. Perry: bass guitar, vocals, percussion
Richard Coughlan: drums, percussion, timpani
Additional personnel:
Rupert Hine: ARP synthesizer on 'Memory Lain, Hugh' / 'Headloss' and 'Be Alright' / 'Chance of a Lifetime'
Frank Ricotti: congas on 'Headloss', Hoedown', 'C'thlu Thlu' and 'L'auberge du Sanglier'
Additional musicians on 'Memory Lain, Hugh' / 'Headloss':
Jimmy Hastings: flute
Pete King: flute, alto saxophone
Harry Klein: clarinet, baritone saxophone
Tony Coe: clarinet, tenor saxophone
Henry Lowther: trumpet
Chris Pyne: trombone
Barry Robinson: piccolo
Tom Whittle: clarinet, tenor saxophone
Jill Pryor: voice on 'C'thlu Thlu'
Paul Buckmaster: electric cello on 'Be All Right'
New Symphonia: orchestra on 'Backwards' / 'A Hunting We Shall Go (reprise)'
Martyn Ford: orchestra arranger, conductor on 'Backwards' / 'A Hunting We Shall Go (reprise)'
John Bell: orchestra arranger on 'Backwards' / 'A Hunting We Shall Go (reprise)'
Produced at Tolling Park Studios, Chipping Norton Recording Studio & Decca Studios, London by David Hitchcock
Recording date: 1973
Release date: 5 October 1973
Record label: Deram
Highest chart places: UK: Did not chart, USA: Did not chart
Running time: 45:43

Although the excellent 1971 album *In the Land of Grey and Pink* is regularly cited as Caravan's finest achievement, for the author, *For Girls Who Grow Plump in the Night* remains a particular favourite. Although chart success in the UK eluded Caravan until 1975, this is one of the seminal releases from one of the definitive bands to emerge from the Canterbury school of progressive rock.

Caravan began their journey in Canterbury itself in January 1968. All four founding members originated from psychedelic pioneers The Wilde Flowers who were active from 1964 to 1967. The Wilde Flowers launched the careers of several key players on the Canterbury scene, including Robert Wyatt,

Kevin Ayers and Hugh Hopper. Four studio albums from Caravan followed, including the aforementioned *In the Land of Grey and Pink* and the equally well-received *Waterloo Lily*, but by the Summer of 1972, the band was in a state of disarray.

Bassist Richard Sinclair and keyboardist Steve Miller attempted to take the band in a jazzier direction which didn't sit well with Caravan's structured style and the pair departed. Guitarist, vocalist Pye Hastings and drummer Richard Coughlan enlisted Geoffrey Richardson, Stu Evans and Derek Austin for touring purposes, with former keyboardist Dave Sinclair making guest appearances. In the Spring of 1973, the line-up underwent another reshuffle with Evans and Austin replaced by bassist John G. Perry and Richard Sinclair's cousin – Dave Sinclair. The latter had left Caravan in August 1971 for a spell in both Matching Mole and Hatfield and the North. This seemingly restless band hopping was typical of many exponents of the Canterbury scene.

When the quintet of Hastings, Coughlan, Perry, Sinclair and Richardson entered the studio to record the fifth album, they were joined by a host of session players, more so than any other Caravan album. Previously, the songs had mostly been credited to the band, but here, Hastings is the principal songwriter and to his credit, he doesn't over-extend himself. In addition to overseeing Caravan's best albums, producer David Hitchcock's pedigree included genre classics *Foxtrot* by Genesis, *The Snow Goose* by Camel and *Scheherazade and Other Stories* by Renaissance.

Caravan's very English sense of humour is evident in the songs and the album artwork. In keeping with the title, when the gatefold sleeve is opened out, the sleeping female figure is revealed to be pregnant. A fully naked variation was photographed and used for promotional purposes but was considered too risqué for the album sleeve. Unfortunately, there is no lyric sheet to capture the band's unique, double entendre wordplay.

Three weeks after the album's release, the band recorded their first live album *Caravan and the New Symphonia*, at London's Theatre Royal, Drury Lane. It was released in April 1974, although ironically, it wasn't until the expanded CD reissue in 2001 that songs from the current album were included. Martyn Ford was again responsible for the orchestrations.

Side one
'Memory Lain, Hugh' 5:00 / 'Headloss' 4:19 (Pye Hastings)

This double header opener gets the album off to a lively start. 'Memory Lain, Hugh' is a mid-tempo rocker, driven by Pye Hastings' incessant trebly guitar chords and Richard Coughlan's shuffle rhythm. Horns and clarinets enter at 1:25 from a line-up of guest musicians that reads like a who's who of traditional British jazz talent. The riff here is not a million miles from 'Boogie Nights', which was an International hit for funk band Heatwave in 1977.

At the three minute mark, a mellow interlude features a flute solo from Pye's brother Jimmy Hastings. Although not a full-time member, Jimmy played on every Caravan album from 1968 to 1976 and was prominent on the Canterbury scene, performing with Soft Machine, Hatfield and the North, and National Health. Highly respected record producer Rupert Hine also adds his ARP synth talents to this track.

'Memory Lain, Hugh' is the story of a man who's not concerned with material wealth, he just wants to go back and rediscover the person he once was. Propelled by Richard Coughlan's powerful drumming, it reaches a crescendo before 'Headloss' takes over at the five-minute mark. The tempo here is faster, but it's another upbeat, guitar-driven song with a touch of wah-wah that borders on boogie rock – with a Canterbury twist, of course. It's almost autobiographical, concerning a musician who's at peace with himself and his love life: 'I've got my pipe and I've got my song, and I've got love to keep me happy'.

'Hoedown' 3:10 (Hastings)

This is not to be confused with Aaron Copland's exuberant slice of Americana of the same name made famous by ELP. That said, the twangy guitar riff does give it an uplifting, vaguely country and western feel, coupled with a Bo Diddley flavoured syncopated rhythm. The chugging congas courtesy of peerless session musician Frank Ricotti are prominent, as is Geoff Richardson's lively viola solo that occupies the midsection instrumental bridge.

This is another song with a personal slant where the freewheeling lyrics match the mood of the music: 'Got a gig I'd like you to know, we're leaving here tonight, we're going just to sing our song and everything's all right'.

'Surprise, Surprise' 4:05 (Hastings)

Following three energetic rockers, the band ease off the accelerator for this stylish offering notable for John G. Perry's articulate bass pattern. This was Perry's only studio album with Caravan, but he distinguishes himself throughout. He would become a respected session musician, playing on several classic 1970s albums by Anthony Phillips and Gordon Giltrap.

It moves up a gear for the upbeat, catchy chorus, but it's mostly a reflective song about a lovestruck romantic who visits an old acquaintance and recalls their past relationship: 'Didn't we believe we were something'. Had they chosen to release a single from the album, this would have been an obvious contender.

'C'thlu Thlu' 6:10 (Hastings)

The subject of this song is the stuff of nightmares: fear of the unknown and being chased through the dark woods by something or someone sinister. The title is an adaptation of 'Cthulhu', a mythical beast created by renowned American horror and fantasy writer H. P. Lovecraft in the 1920s.

In keeping with the theme, it has a macabre atmosphere with ominous, plodding guitar chords, spooky electronic effects and Jill Pryor's ghostly, siren-like voice. The choral hook, however, has a buoyant charm before Hastings unleashes a discordant guitar solo at 3:25. A relentless riff underpins David

Sinclair's eerie synth and organ effects before he cuts loose with a blistering solo – the song's highpoint. Crashing chords bring the song and the first side to a chilling finish.

Side two
'The Dog, the Dog, He's At It Again' 5:53 (Hastings)

If side one demonstrates Caravan's mainstream rock sensibilities, side two is a showcase for their progressive credentials. It begins with the album's most memorable song and one of Caravan's best ever. It boasts a beautiful arrangement with Hastings' engaging – as opposed to forceful – vocal in its element with superlative harmonies and a choral hook to die for.

As the title suggests, this is a tongue-in-cheek song about carnal lust, as evident in the memorable lines: 'My mother said that I should stay out of bed, but I know that I like it in there'. In the perverted mind of the randy protagonist, sex is the equivalent of a medical cure.

For the instrumental bridge, Sinclair turns in a noodly synth solo that literally screams the high notes. For his part, Richardson provides a lovely viola backdrop for the verses. The final chorus with its infectious counterpoint harmonies is stunning.

Although Richardson left Caravan in 1978, he returned and along with Hastings, he's the only surviving member from this period. On the band's website, they announced the release of their latest album, *It's None Of Your Business,* in October 2021, their first in eight years.

'Be All Right' / 'Chance of a Lifetime' 6:38 (Hastings)

Like the album opener, this is another pairing, only this time with two very contrasting songs. The rhythmic intro mimics the sound of a speeding train, joined by a compelling riff with Paul Buckmaster's vibrant electric cello doubling guitar. It careers along at a breakneck pace with a soaring solo from Hastings and another of his memorable choruses, although on this occasion, it's sung by the rawer voiced Perry. 'Be All Right' is a celebration of love and the joy that it can bring whilst disparaging the world's dependency on monetary values.

At 2:30, it eases into the mellow groove of 'Chance of a Lifetime' with light percussion backing Hastings' wistful vocal. It's a lovely song with a simple message: happiness is a mindset, so look on the positive side of life – 'Look for the sunrise'. The instrumental break features a delightful, close-miked viola solo in the instrumental break and superb lead-line bass playing from Perry.

'L'auberge du Sanglier' / 'A Hunting We Shall Go' / 'Pengola' / 'Backwards' / 'A Hunting We Shall Go (reprise)' 10:03
(Hastings, John G. Perry, Mike Ratledge)

This five-part, ten-minute instrumental suite provides a fitting finale. Opening with 'L'auberge du Sanglier' – which translates into English as 'The wild boar inn' – it features a rare moment of solo acoustic guitar with graceful viola weaving in and out. It's the lull before the storm, however, and following a cymbal ride, it literally explodes into the restless 'A Hunting We Shall Go'.

The title is based on the popular eighteenth-century nursery rhyme 'A-Hunting We Will Go', but this pounding instrumental, with its tricky twists and turns, jagged power chords and rhythmic punctuations, is anything but benign. It's tunefully compelling, however, featuring the album's best playing with superb bass and guitar exchanges and a stunning viola solo. Perry is responsible for the 'Pengola' sequence.

At 4:30, it dissolves into 'Backwards', a lush, romantic instrumental with piano and synth backed by soaring strings and brass courtesy of the New Symphonia under the skilled direction of Martyn Ford. As the orchestra soars skywards, it has a distinct John Barry flavour and, despite the dense arrangement, the drums and bass are superbly distinct throughout. 'Backwards' was written by Soft Machine's keyboardist Mike Ratledge and originally featured on their *Third* album as part of the side-long medley 'Slightly All the Time'.

A short reprise of 'A Hunting We Shall Go' is augmented by the orchestra before all too soon; a crash of thunder brings things to an abrupt conclusion.

Genesis – *Selling England by the Pound*

Personnel:
Phil Collins: drums, percussion, lead vocal on 'More Fool Me', backing vocals
Michael Rutherford: twelve-string, bass, electric sitar
Stephen Hackett: electric guitar, nylon guitar
Tony Banks: keyboards, twelve-string
Peter Gabriel: vocals, flute, oboe, percussion
Produced at Island Studios, London by John Burns & Genesis
Recording date: August 1973
Release date: 13 October 1973
Record label: Charisma
Highest chart places: UK: 3, USA: 70, Italy: 4
Running time: 53:44

In 1973, the Peter Gabriel era Genesis was in the middle of a creative, three-album hot streak that began with *Foxtrot* in 1972 and culminated with *The Lamb Lies Down on Broadway* in 1974. On its initial release, however, some fans and critics were ambivalent towards *Selling England by the Pound*, feeling it lacked the dynamics of previous albums, especially *Foxtrot*. In more recent times, it's come to be regarded as the band's finest work and regularly scores highly in album polls. In 2007, it topped *Prog Rock* magazine's list of 'Top 30 Prog Rock Albums'.

In his autobiography *The Living Years*, Mike Rutherford admitted that: 'The album was difficult to write because *Foxtrot* had been so successful'.

Much of it was written in an old country house in Chessington, south of London, a district better known for its zoo. Rather than contributing individual parts and stitching them together as was their customary practice, they attempted lengthy group jams, although these did not always bear fruit. To buy the band more time, Charisma Records released *Genesis Live* as a stopgap which peaked at a healthy number nine in the UK chart on 11 August 1973. They also took time out to headline the Reading Festival in the south of England on Sunday, 26 August.

An eight-month world tour followed, opening in Paris on 19 September, and it was the band's most successful to date – especially in America, which had been slow to warm to Genesis. The stage backdrop was one of the most subtle and effective I witnessed in the early 1970s, featuring white gauze screens illuminated by UV lights that hid the amp and speaker cabinets.

On 20 October 1973, the second of two sell-out shows at London's Rainbow Theatre was filmed for a possible cinema release that never materialised, although footage circulates amongst collectors and can be viewed on YouTube. On the same day, one week after its release, *Selling England by the Pound* peaked at number 3 in the UK, their highest-charting album by far up to that point. It was also the band's first entry on the American Billboard chart. It charted highly in Italy, one of the first countries to embrace the music of Genesis, and in Rome on 5 February 1974, they performed in front of 20,000 ecstatic fans.

Although *Selling England by the Pound* isn't a concept album per se, Peter Gabriel described the underlying theme to several songs as the 'Commercialisation of English culture'. Throughout, the singer is in his role-playing element and his lyrics are ripe with wordplay, whimsy and cynicism. He's in fine vocal form; the now-familiar rasp was still several solo albums away. Like the previous albums, the songs were credited to the whole band, but Tony Banks was already asserting himself as the principal songwriter. It was Phil Collins and Steve Hackett's third studio outing with Genesis and, along with Mike Rutherford, their playing was noticeably more fluid and adventurous. Banks plays synthesizer for the first time on record, although his instrument of choice is the ARP Pro Soloist rather than the Minimoog favoured by his contemporaries.

Artist Betty Swanwick's painting 'The Dream' inspired Gabriel's lyrics for the song 'I Know What I Like' when he saw it hanging in a gallery. At the band's request, she added a lawnmower next to the sleeping figure when it was enlarged for the album cover.

Side one

'Dancing with the Moonlit Knight' 8:04 (Tony Banks, Phil Collins, Peter Gabriel, Steve Hackett, Mike Rutherford)

In contrast to the gothic Mellotron chords of 'Watcher of the Skies' that opened the previous album, Gabriel's unaccompanied 'Can you tell me where my country lies' harks back to the acapella line 'Looking for someone' that opened the 1970 album *Trespass*. He's searching for an England from a bygone age before modernity and commercialism took hold. During the subsequent tour, Gabriel performed the song dressed as Britannia, complete with helmet, trident and shield.

The song boasts a strong melody and encompasses a variety of styles, including rock, folk, classical and jazz fusion. There's a touch of Scottish plainsong and Elgar in the opening verses, Mozart influences in the rising Mellotron choir and a fast guitar riff worthy of Prokofiev. Hackett's soloing incorporates several trademark techniques, including string tapping, sweep picking and octave leaps. Banks' ARP synth makes its debut appearance on a Genesis album, although the more familiar timbre of the Hammond organ is never far away. Rutherford contributes inventive chord progressions and the stop-start rhythms are an indication that Collins had been listening to the Mahavishnu Orchestra, channelling Billy Cobham's complex patterns. During the rapid-fire verses, Gabriel's words almost trip up over themselves, trying to keep up.

'I Know What I Like (In Your Wardrobe)' 4:08 (Banks, Collins, Gabriel, Hackett, Rutherford)

Based on a guitar riff, this song originated from Hackett and Collins and was initially rejected by the band before becoming a popular live staple. Musically, it embodies the whimsical spirit of Gabriel's tale of a shiftless gardener who ignores the advice of friends and neighbours to better himself. The line 'There's a future for you in the fire escape trade' is a reference to illegal gambling in 1920s America, where the fire escape provided a quick exit in the event of police raids.

When it was released as a single the following year, it was a surprise hit, reaching number 21 in the UK singles chart in April 1974. The band turned down an offer to appear on the weekly TV show *Top of the Pops,* believing it would compromise their integrity, much to manager Tony Stratton-Smith's frustration.

When it was performed live, Gabriel delivered the spoken intro in a mock southwest country drawl and would then push an invisible lawnmower across the stage with a piece of straw gripped between his teeth. Following his departure, it would form the basis for a medley of older tunes, while during Hackett's recent solo shows, it has developed into an extended jam.

'Firth of Fifth' 9:38 (Banks, Collins, Gabriel, Hackett, Rutherford)

A leftover from the *Foxtrot* sessions, Banks was mostly responsible for this song, although Rutherford contributed to the lyrics. The words are secondary, however. Banks' real forte are the instrumental set pieces, hooks and melodic motifs and this is evident on 'Firth of Fifth'. It opens with a rare – for Genesis – piano solo establishing the main theme. When it was performed on the *Selling England by the Pound* tour, the intro was omitted during the 1973 leg but was reinstated in January 1974. Banks wrestled with the electric piano, including the occasional bum note and there was a noticeable pause as he transferred to organ before the rest of the band came crashing in.

The stately vocal melody is delivered with suitable gravitas by Gabriel before exchanging his vocal cords for flute. As the music swells during the piano section, there's a real sense of anticipation, and Banks delivers with an uplifting synth solo that reprises the piano theme. This could have been the standout part, but 'Firth of Fifth' is best remembered for Hackett's iconic, sustain drenched solo that dominates the second half. It's a development of the flute melody and was assembled from three separate guitar takes played back together. It always brought the house down when performed live with Genesis – even though Hackett remained seated – and continues to do so in his solo shows.

'More Fool Me' 3:10 (Banks, Collins, Gabriel, Hackett, Rutherford)

Collins penned the words and Rutherford the music for this wistful ballad and it was the first song they wrote together. It's also a rarity for Genesis from this period – a conventional love song. More specifically, it's a tale of a relationship on the rocks that would be echoed in Collins' later work, especially his 1981 debut *Face Value* recorded following the breakdown of his marriage. The sparse twelve-string guitar backing is perfect for his melancholic vocal.

'More Fool Me' was only the second lead vocal outing for Collins, following the equally lyrical 'For Absent Friends' on Genesis' *Nursery Cryme* in 1971. Until the sessions for *A Trick of the Tail* in 1975, the general perception was that his voice was only suited to ballads even though he backed Gabriel on many of the band's songs.

When it was performed during the subsequent tour, Collins would emerge from behind his drum kit to rapturous applause. In contrast with Gabriel's theatrical demeanour, Collins usually sang with his hands thrust in his pockets and always received a standing ovation, responding with a humble 'thankyou'.

Side two
'The Battle of Epping Forest' 11:46 (Banks, Collins, Gabriel, Hackett, Rutherford)

Like many songwriters, Gabriel looked to various sources for inspiration, including the news media. This mini-epic that opens side two is based on a true-life account of two rival crime gangs fighting over territorial protection rights in London's east end. When the instrumental track was recorded, the rest of the band were pleased with the results but believed the music and the lyrics were ill-matched. Despite the subject, the music remains in familiar melodic Genesis territory, although for the next album, Gabriel's surreal story of a New York street punk, they developed a leaner, harder sound.

Gabriel's tongue-in-cheek saga combines whimsy and cynicism with a succession of dubious but hilariously named characters. His comical vocal mannerisms include a camp inflection for 'Harold Demure', a pious tone for 'the Reverend' and a mock cockney accent for 'Mick the Prick'. To get into character when the song was performed live, he wore a stocking mask over his head while prancing gleefully around the stage.

Despite the band's misgivings, the music provides a suitably dramatic soundtrack as the story unfolds and is full of inspired moments. These include an introductory march, inventive guitar and organ fills, a celestial interlude for the Reverend, a memorable choral hook, majestic synth trills and a strong finale. Throughout, Collins' tricky but relentless drumming is phenomenal.

'After the Ordeal' 4:16 (Banks, Collins, Gabriel, Hackett, Rutherford)

This aptly titled instrumental is the lull after the storm. Like all the material on the album, it was credited to the band even though it's a Hackett composition with contributions from Rutherford. Banks did not want it included, however, possibly because he was dissatisfied with his own performance, which, in Armando Gallo's book *Genesis: I Know What I Like*, he described as 'atrocious'.

Ever the perfectionist, Banks is doing himself an injustice. The opening section, a piano and classical guitar duet, is very ornate, beautifully played and quite unlike anything else recorded by the band before or since. At the halfway mark, Banks' crashing chords introduce Hackett's stately electric guitar lament. It's a lovely theme with a touch of flute to play out.

'After the Ordeal' was not the first – and it would not be the last – time Hackett had to fight his corner over the inclusion of one of his compositions, although on this occasion, he won the argument. It was the success of his solo album *Voyage of the Acolyte* in 1975 that sowed the seeds for his departure in 1977.

'The Cinema Show' 11:06 (Banks, Collins, Gabriel, Hackett, Rutherford)

The penultimate track is in two distinct parts. The first is a song in the classic Genesis mould with twelve-string guitar, fine harmonies, Gabriel's woodwind embellishments and Hackett's soaring lead lines elevating a more than decent vocal melody.

Although the protagonists are named Romeo and Juliet, the song is less an update on William Shakespeare than it is T.S. Eliot's 1922 poem *The Waste Land*. In part three, 'The Fire Sermon', Eliot describes a sexual liaison: 'Exploring hands encounter no defence' and adds: 'And I Tiresias have foresuffered all, Enacted on this same divan or bed'. Tiresias is a prophet in Greek mythology and one of literature's first transsexuals. In 'The Cinema Show' bridge which occurs twice in the song, he is 'Father Tiresias' and recalls 'Once a man, like the sea I raged, Once a woman, like the earth I gave'. Genesis also turn Eliot's line 'A Bradford millionaire' – a self-made man from a working-class background – into 'A weekend millionaire' to describe Romeo who has his own aspirations: 'I will make my bed with her tonight, he cries'.

When performed live on the subsequent tour, Gabriel would exit the stage after delivering the final line, followed by Hackett. As such, the near five-minute instrumental sequence that follows is a prophetic foretaste of things to come. Driven by Collins' powerful 7/8 rhythm, Banks' synth workout is a masterclass in tasteful technique, improvising over Rutherford's inventive chords. It was resurrected in 2021 for *The Last Domino?* tour and, ripe with melody and harmonic development, it draws on modern classical music and fusion before segueing into...

'Aisle of Plenty' 1:32 (Banks, Collins, Gabriel, Hackett, Rutherford)

'Aisle of Plenty' is a double meaning allusion to the British Isles as a land of plenty and the well-stocked aisles of a supermarket. To ram home the message, Gabriel's prose is ripe with thinly veiled references to famous UK food brands and retail chains, although this being 1973, some have long since gone out of business. The Mellotron choir, guitar and rhythm repeat is lifted from 'Dancing with the Moonlit Knight', bringing the album full circle.

Emerson Lake & Palmer – *Brain Salad Surgery*

Personnel:
Keith Emerson: organs, piano, harpsichord, accordion, custom-built Moog
synthesizers, Moog Polyphonic Ensemble
Greg Lake: vocals, bass, Semites electric six-string & twelve-string guitars
Carl Palmer: drums, percussion, percussion synthesizers
Produced at Olympic Studios and Advision Studios, London by Greg Lake
Recording date: June to September 1973
UK release date: 19 November 1973, US release date: 12 December 1973
Record label: Manticore
Highest chart places: UK: 2, USA: 11
Running time: 45:02

Like Genesis' *Selling England by the Pound*, Emerson Lake & Palmer's fifth
album received a mixed reception when first released but is now generally
regarded as their crowning achievement. It's certainly their best known and
best-selling offering, due in no small part to Swiss artist H.R. Giger's gothic
cover artwork. The album encompasses every aspect of ELP's musical persona,
including bombast, humour and virtuoso playing, loved by fans and despised
by naysayers in almost equal measures. One thing that struck me as a prog fan
in the 1970s, if you liked Yes, then it was generally accepted that you also liked
Genesis and King Crimson, but when it came to ELP, opinions were divided.
For the record, I have all their albums on vinyl which makes it pretty clear
where my loyalties lie.

At the beginning of 1973, ELP formed their own record label, Manticore
and signed a handful of like-minded acts whose music they identified with,
including Pete Sinfield. Following the ambitious *Get Me a Ladder* tour of
Europe in the Spring, they adjourned to the studio to begin work on *Brain
Salad Surgery*. Although several songs had been road-tested, including *Toccata*
and *Karn Evil 9*, the protracted recording process resulted in the release date
being postponed several times. Keith Emerson later reflected: 'I think it was
worth the wait because a lot of people think *Brain Salad Surgery* is just about
the best thing we ever did'.

In November, just over a week before the release, *NME* readers in the UK
were given a taster of sorts with a free flexi disc that featured the namesake
song 'Brain Salad Surgery' although it was hardly representative of the album.
Ironically, the flexi disc sleeve is a higher resolution than the hazy album
artwork upon which it's based. The album title, which doesn't appear on the
cover, was lifted from Dr John's song 'Right Place, Wrong Time'.

Although sonically *Brain Salad Surgery* is quite different from previous
albums, mainly thanks to Greg Lake's clinical production, structurally, it follows
a now-familiar pattern. There's a cover of a classical piece, a semi-acoustic
ballad, a tongue-in-cheek romp – typically the weakest track – and an epic
length centrepiece.

Brain Salad Surgery peaked at number 2 in the UK on 30 December, one place behind *Tales from Topographic Oceans*. With Yes and ELP topping the album chart, New Year's Eve 1973 was a memorable one for prog fans. The band's version of 'Jerusalem' was also ideal material for the Christmas market, but when it was released as a single on 30 November, the BBC considered a rock version of the unofficial English anthem inappropriate and, as they monopolised the UK airwaves, the subsequent radio ban resulted in poor sales.

Five days before the album's UK release, the band hit the road once more. It was one of their longest and most prestigious tours to date, crisscrossing North America before a handful of UK dates in April 1974. The subsequent triple live LP *Welcome Back, My Friends, to the Show That Never Ends – Ladies and Gentlemen* (August 1974) includes every song from the album with the exception of the dispensable 'Benny the Bouncer'. ELP were at the peak of their powers, but fans would have to wait until 1977 before the next album, to be their most extravagant undertaking yet.

Side one
'Jerusalem' 2:44 (William Blake, Hubert Parry)
It's hard to imagine that ELP's rendition of this popular hymn rankled the powers that be at the BBC back in 1973. At under three minutes, it's radio-friendly and tastefully executed. Blake's prose is based on a supposition that Christ once visited England and set to Parry's triumphant music; it has become a symbol of nationalistic pride.

ELP's version remains faithful to the traditional arrangement, full of pomp and circumstance and Lake singing with suitable, echo-drenched gusto. The opening chord progression is similar to *Pictures at an Exhibition* with Hammond organ leading the way and Palmer embellishing with tubular bells, tympani rolls and a crashing gong. The synth parps during the chorus are suitably regal; Moog's newly developed polyphonic synthesizer makes its debut here, which Emerson also put to good use on 'Toccata' and 'Benny the Bouncer'.

Although 'Jerusalem' was not a Christmas hit, Lake scored two years later when his solo single 'I Believe in Father Christmas' peaked at number two in the UK chart over the 1975 festive holidays.

'Toccata' 7:23 (Alberto Ginastera)
Emerson was introduced to Ginastera's 'Piano Concerto No.1' in February 1970 when The Nice and several other notable acts performed at the *Switched On Symphony* event in California. It was performed by a Brazilian pianist with the Los Angeles Philharmonic Orchestra and Emerson was suitably impressed. With pounding piano, it was already a very percussive piece to begin with, which ELP developed on their adaptation of the fourth movement, 'Toccata concertata'.

Although they performed the piece on the European tour in the Spring of 1973, it was necessary to contact the composer personally to obtain permission

111

before committing it to record. During his time with The Nice and ELP, Emerson adapted the work of several 20th-century composers who were still very much alive at the time.

Tympani begins proceedings before organ and bass come crashing into view, rampaging through the opening sequence. This is ELP at their most muscular and the repeated theme beginning at 2:16 echoes 'Abaddon's Bolero' on the previous album. At the three-minute mark, Palmer's extended percussion movement incorporates traditional tuned instruments before unleashing Moog's experimental drum synth for a sequence of ear-piercing electronic effects.

'Still... You Turn Me On' 2:53 (Greg Lake)

It was by now a common feature of ELP albums to include a mostly solo offering from Lake to balance the grandiose ambitions of Emerson's compositions and adaptations. Along with 'Lucky Man', and 'Take a Pebble', this is one of Lake's best-known contributions to the band and one of his finest songs ever. The lyrics can be interpreted in two ways; Lake is speaking to a loved one, or he's addressing his audience. Either way, he sings from the heart.

Lake's rippling acoustic guitar is enriched by Emerson's accordion, harpsichord and a touch of synth. Funky, wah-wah guitar punctuates the chorus and disrupts the calm but is a welcome intrusion nonetheless. The song was considered for a single release, but Emerson and Palmer refused as it wasn't representative of the band.

That same year, Lake recorded the similarly titled 'Still' with Pete Sinfield, which was the title track on the latter's solo album. Sinfield reciprocated Lake's involvement and the patronage of Manticore by agreeing to contribute lyrics for this album, including the next song.

'Benny the Bouncer' 2:21 (Lake, Pete Sinfield, Keith Emerson)

Perhaps as a reaction to critics to prove they didn't take themselves too seriously, ELP seemed compelled to include a novelty song on each album. With its honky-tonk piano, 'Benny the Bouncer' follows in the same irreverent footsteps as 'The Sheriff' on *Trilogy* and 'Are You Ready, Eddy' on *Tarkus*.

It's hard to believe that it took the combined talents of Sinfield and Lake to pen lines like 'Sidney grabbed a hatchet, buried it in Benny's head' with the latter singing in an aggressive 'mockney' accent. There's obvious parallels between this song and 'Ernie', a 1971 hit for British comedian Benny Hill. In addition to the 'Benny' connection, the subject of both songs is a fight between two rivals that results in the demise of the title character. And compare, for example, Hill's line 'A stale pork pie caught him in the eye' with ELP's 'Benny got a cold meat pie'.

Thankfully, at less than two-and-a-half minutes, it doesn't outstay its welcome.

'Karn Evil 9: 1st Impression – Part 1' 8:44 (Lake, Emerson)

This was the first track recorded for the album and due to the constraints of vinyl, it's divorced from the rest of the piece, which occupies side two. When reissued on CD, 'Karn Evil 9' became a continuous 30-minute work. The concept of mankind in conflict with the superior machines and computers he has created is the stuff of sci-fi films like *Blade Runner* and the *Terminator* franchise. The title is a play on the word 'carnival' and was devised by Sinfield, reflecting his impression of the music.

Lake's opening verses set the scene of a desolate future world where people are suffering but seemingly there is a saviour at hand – 'I'll be there!'. The music is strident, with jangling percussion accompanying the verses. Emerson plays organ for the most part, with synth providing embellishments and fills, establishing the main theme of the piece. A rapid instrumental break introduces a second but equally memorable synth melody while Lake and Palmer's manipulation of the convoluted time signatures is a wonder to behold.

Beginning with organ stabs, the second vocal melody is more upbeat, with Lake enthusiastically describing a bizarre collection of exhibits in a carnival show. The instrumental theme returns to provide a majestic finale to this wonderful, fully contained track, but there's more to come.

Side two
'Karn Evil 9: 1st Impression – Part 2' 4:47 (Lake, Emerson)

To open side two, bubbling synth underpins Lake's rousing 'Welcome back my friends, to the show that never ends', which would become the band's signature. Sinfield later asserted that it was he, and not Lake, that was responsible for the line. It acts as a link to part one, continuing the same lyrical theme with Lake adopting the role of a hawker inviting his audience to see the show.

Hammond organ is once again front and centre, propelled by Palmer's shuffle rhythm and Lake's gymnastic bass lines and guitar fills. The stunning organ solo is a throwback to the days of The Nice, with soaring Moog maintaining a reminder of the principal theme. The carnival atmosphere is maintained with Palmer throwing in superb drum volleys before the bombastic ending, which always brought the house down when performed live.

'Karn Evil 9: 2nd Impression' 7:07 (Emerson)

The second movement is entirely instrumental, which Emerson describes as a series of abstracts that deal with the disorientating effects of time and travel.

Here, virtuoso piano takes the lead and, coupled with the busy drumming, it has a lively jazz-rock swing. At 1:10, Emerson uses the Minimoog to mimic the calypso sound of a steel drum, which enhances the carnival atmosphere established in the first impression. At 2:22, there's a blink-and-you-miss-it snippet from Sonny Rollins' 1956 jazz standard 'St. Thomas' before the piano comes cascading back in.

113

At 2:51, the music comes to a dead stop. Slowly, an eerie, impressionistic sequence unfolds with ELP at their most avant-garde. At 5:43, piano once again hits its energetic stride and muscles its way through an impressive jazz workout, combining composed and improvised music in equal measures. The synchronicity between piano, bass and drums is extraordinary, and it's no surprise that at his peak in the 1970s, Emerson regularly topped the 'best keyboardist' polls.

'Karn Evil 9: 3rd Impression' 9:03 (Lake, Sinfield, Emerson)

With Sinfield assisting Lake with the lyrics, the final movement focuses on the revolt of the computers and their battle for supremacy with mankind. Although there is no obvious narrative link with the '1st Impression', the musical themes introduced in part one are reprised.

It's suitably audacious from the start as man boasts his superiority over all things. Lake is in his element singing this heroic type of song, which would be echoed in 'Pirates' in 1977. He receives empathetic support from Emerson's majestic synth melody and Palmer's inventive drumming. The commanding line 'No one yields who flies in my ship' is powerfully effective, while the noble instrumental theme at 2:55 is the lull before the storm. At 4:30, the instrumental bridge dominated by frantic Hammond soloing provides the soundtrack to the raging battle that ensues before staccato chords announce that a resolution is at hand.

At 7:35, man rejoices in his victory, but the computer asserts its supremacy with the final chilling line, 'I'm perfect, are you?' Emerson provides the voice of the computer, which was processed through his modular Moog. Following apocalyptic crashing chords, at 8:30, the Moog's sequencer plays an ascending chain of notes, darting between the left and right speakers, which, on stage, would bring the piece to an explosive finale.

Nektar – *Remember the Future*

Personnel:
Allan 'Taff' Freeman: keyboards, backing vocals
Roye Albrighton: guitars, lead vocals
Derek 'Mo' Moore: bass guitar, backing vocals
Ron Howden: drums, percussion, backing vocals
Produced at Chipping Norton Studios, Oxfordshire, England by Nektar and Peter
Hauke Recording date: August 1973
Release date: 23 November 1973
Record label: United Artists
Highest chart places: UK: Did not chart, USA: 19, Australia: 72
Running time: 35:40

Nektar formed in Hamburg in 1969 and this, coupled with the Germanic
spelling of their name, led to the popular misconception that they were a
German band. They are, in fact, all English, namely the late Roye Albrighton
(guitars, lead vocals), Allan Freeman (keyboards), Derek Moore (bass) and Ron
Howden (drums). Nektar also credited their lighting technician Mick Brockett
as a band member, not unlike Genesis, who had a similar regard for their
sound engineer Richard MacPhail. The original line-up lasted until 1976 and
recorded six studio albums.

Following hot on the heels of the previous album ...*Sounds Like This*,
Remember the Future was released in Europe in 1973 and is Nektar's most
acclaimed work. It was their first studio recording in the UK; the three previous
albums were all recorded in Germany. Nektar based themselves in the heart
of Germany south of Frankfurt and in 1973, they toured locally as well as
Switzerland, France, Austria and several visits to the UK presenting their 'Music
and Light Theatre'. They were also the opening act on Frank Zappa's European
tour.

Nektar recorded an hour-long concert for Swiss TV and this – along with a
performance at the Pavilion des Sports in Lausanne in May 1973 – was released
in 2021 as *Sounds Like Swiss*. Material recorded live on 25 November featured
on the 1974 album *Sunday Night at the London Roundhouse*. In 1974, they
toured America and Europe and in July that year, I saw them at the Penzance
Winter Gardens, Cornwall, in the southwest of England. As I recall, I enjoyed
the gig, but then again, I was on holiday at the time and the beer was flowing
freely.

Remember the Future proved to be very popular in America when it
appeared there in 1974. The fact that it breached the Billboard top twenty is a
remarkable achievement given that the band hadn't previously toured the USA.
They were no strangers to American soil, however; in the summer of 1970,
they recorded their first studio tapes in the Jamaica Plain district of Boston,
Massachusetts, for an intended album that failed to materialise. Several songs
were reworked for the ...*Sounds Like This* album, but the original tapes were

115

thought to be lost. They were unearthed for the 40th-anniversary reissue of *Remember the Future* and are included on the bonus CD as *The 1970 Boston Tapes*, which features eight previously unreleased songs.

Remember the Future is a concept album – naturally – about a winged alien called Bluebird with telepathic powers who is rejected on Earth because of his colour but befriends a blind boy. Guitarist Roye Albrighton takes up the story:

> Being blind meant that the boy would have no misconceptions about who he was talking to. Bluebird tells him of the wonders and pitfalls that humans will go through before their evolution is complete.

German illustrator Helmut Wenske produced the album artwork before he had any knowledge of the Bluebird concept, but it fitted perfectly with the band's vision. By sheer coincidence, the painting on the rear cover features blue-winged creatures that are half-man and half bat-like in appearance. It's one of several stunning creations by Wenske for the band and the fantasy imagery went hand in hand with their psychedelic stage productions.

Side one
'Remember the Future (Part I)': a) 'Images of the Past', b) 'Wheel of Time', c) 'Remember the Future', d) 'Confusion'
16:38 (Nektar)

When *Remember the Future* was first released on vinyl in November 1973, it was simply listed as 'Part 1' on side one and 'Part 2' on side two. It was only on later CD reissues that each part was sub-divided into separately titled sections, which I've taken the liberty of including here. Although each part plays as one continuous piece of music, it's evident that it was assembled from individually composed and recorded sections. In part one, for example, the title song 'Remember the Future' fades out before the instrumental 'Confusion' fades back in.

Compared with many of the albums in this section of the book, *Remember the Future* is a relatively undemanding, tuneful work and each part seems to go by in a flash, which is always a positive sign. Although fans may disagree, it's relatively prog-lite, suggesting that Nektar's progressive rock tag has as much to do with the sci-fi imagery – album title, concept, artwork and stage show – as it does the music. Melodic space rock with traces of blues, funk, prog and The Beatles in their psychedelic phase would be a more apt description. Despite the 1973 production values, it could just as easily be a product of the late 1960s.

Nonetheless, the individual sections are certainly entertaining with memorable hooks and catchy vocal melodies where Albrighton's engaging lead vocal is supported by strong block harmonies from Freeman, Moore and Howden. Together, they produce a distinct, west-coast sound – that's California, not Cornwall – à la Crosby, Stills, Nash & Young.

The inner album sleeve provides a synopsis for each of the two parts as well as the lyrics. In part one, Bluebird looks back in time and using telepathy, he provides the young boy with a vision of man's evolution and his future as well as an image of himself: 'And now that you've seen me, I see it's behind you, Remember the future will always be there'. Although he's unafraid, the boy is confused by the visions.

Musically, part one eschews soloing in favour of extended riffs and fills to support the narrative. It has a sunny, upbeat vibe for the most part, with wah-wah guitar leading into a jangly refrain to accompany the jaunty vocal melody. A six-note organ motif underpins the chant-like verses while fuzzed guitar chords contrast nicely with harmonised vocals. As the song builds, a twangy riff propels the ascending 'Remember the Future' choral hook. The spacey, instrumental coda is awash with repeated organ and bass chords, an imaginative drum pattern and discordant guitar histrionics.

Compared with the original, the 40th Anniversary Edition of *Remember the Future* has a cleaner sound, although Freeman's keyboards seem to have gone AWOL during the transfer. When they do surface, his Hammond arpeggios are a delight. Albrighton's guitar versatility covers a good deal of ground, echoing amongst others Pete Townshend's power chords, Jimi Hendrix's bluesy jams, David Gilmour's melodic phrasing and Tom Johnston's – of The Doobie Brothers fame – chugging funk riffs. Supported by the powerhouse rhythm section of Moore and Howden, the heavier moments have shades of Cream and Rory Gallagher.

Side two
'Remember the Future (Part 2)': e) 'Returning Light', f) 'Questions and Answers', g) 'Tomorrow Never Comes', h) 'Path of Light', i) 'Recognition', j) 'Let it Grow' 18:55 (Nektar)

In part two, the arrangements are more expansive and a touch more progressive. It's also more cohesive with each section complementing the one that has gone before. In contrast to the discussion of part one, I've divided part two into its component sections with a track timing for the start of each based on my reading of the music and lyrics.

'Returning Light': Bluebird grants his new friend the power of sight and the boy is able to see him for the first time. It opens with gentle picked acoustic guitar where the chord progression brings James Taylor's version of 'You've got a Friend' to mind. The mood is broken by punchy power chords with a searing guitar figure and Howden's rapid, martial beat.

'Questions and Answers': The boy asks many questions and in return, Bluebird passes on his knowledge. At 1:45, double-tracked acoustic guitars each play a variation of the same breezy melody. It breaks into an upbeat vocal sequence with vibrant wordless harmonies. The double-time shuffle rhythm is superb, as is the funky guitar refrain. Moore's bass takes the lead, supported by Albrighton's guitar fills. It comes to a calming conclusion with a repeated choral refrain before...

'Tomorrow Never Comes': It kicks up its heels at 7:41 for a rapid but still melodic groove, driven by bass with keyboards providing supportive rhythmic pulses. The combined voices elevate the memorable choral hook to a harmonious peak.

'Path of Light': At 9:00, rippling guitar with a touch of organ provides a moment of peace and tranquillity that evokes *Misplaced Childhood* era Marillion. The light as a feather rhythm complements Albrighton's reflective vocal while his sweet, slow-blues guitar fills and soaring solo would make David Gilmour proud. It's an album highlight.

'Recognition': At 13:20, we take a detour into American funk territory. The drums and bass pattern is infectious and when it hits the surging chorus, Albrighton's soulful singing has all the hallmarks of the late, great Steve Marriott. The wah-wah guitar in the funky middle eight on the other hand, is pure Isaac Hayes.

'Let it Grow': As Bluebird departs, the boy's newfound wisdom allows him to understand the past and look to the future: 'The laws of nature are to heal the wounds of man, Use them right and they will help you if they can'. At 16:20, we're on the home straight with an exhilarating guitar and bass jam. The counterpoint verses and powerful chorus subside into a serene conclusion with a touch of spacey effects to signify Bluebird's departure.

Remember the Future was well received on the 1973 – 1974 tour, and when the original line-up reformed in 2000, it was played in its entirety, as evidenced on the NEARfest 2002 concert DVD. Following Roye Albrighton's death in 2016, the band fragmented, but in 2019, the Derek Moore and Ron Howden rhythm section – along with lighting tech Mick Brockett – put the band back together again. *The Vinyl Sides Live Tour* scheduled for 2022 includes dates across America.

Manfred Mann's Earth Band – *Solar Fire*

Personnel:
Manfred Mann: Hammond B-3 organ, Mellotron, Minimoog synthesiser, lead vocal
on 'Earth, the Circle Part 1'
Mick Rogers: lead vocals, lead & rhythm guitars
Colin Pattenden: bass guitar
Chris Slade: drums
Additional personnel:
Irene Chanter: backing vocals
Doreen Chanter: backing vocals
Grove Singers: backing vocals
Paul Rutherford: trombone
Peter Miles: additional percussion on 'In the Beginning, Darkness'
Produced at The Workhouse Studios, London by Manfred Mann's Earth Band
Recording date: 1973
Release date: 30 November 1973
Record label: Bronze
Highest chart places: UK: Did not chart, USA: 96, Canada: 96
Running time: 37:10

Solar Fire is Manfred Mann's Earth Band's fourth album and their second of
1973, preceded by *Messin'* five months earlier. This is the more adventurous
and proggy of the pair and is a concept based on the planetary system. Gustav
Holst beat them to the draw by some 55 years with *The Planets* suite, which the
band had intended to adapt but was declined permission by the composer's
estate. One song did survive – 'Joybringer' – a punchy update of Holst's
'Jupiter, the Bringer of Jollity'. Although it didn't appear on the original UK
LP of *Solar Fire*, 'Joybringer' was a top ten single in September – Mann's first
since a run of hits in the 1960s. Manfred Mann's 1966 hit 'Pretty Flamingo'
was the first record I purchased with my own pocket money and thanks to my
small contribution, it reached number 1 in the UK the same week as my twelfth
birthday.

Following the demise of Manfred Mann – the band not the man – in 1969,
Mann formed Manfred Mann Chapter Three as a jazz-rock experiment, but the
band faltered in 1971 following two albums. Mann assembled a new line-up
and they released an excellent version of Randy Newman's 'Living Without
You', which also featured on the eponymous *Manfred Mann's Earth Band*
debut album in 1972. The four-piece line-up remained intact for *Solar Fire* and
the following two albums. Six albums in three and half years was no mean feat
– even in the early 1970s – but surprisingly, none charted in the UK.

When guitarist Mick Rogers left the band, the usual musical differences
were cited and he had also received an offer to play with Frank Zappa. Rogers
later said, 'I became too much for the band and I think I had to go'. He was
a major player in the band's development, seamlessly combining pop, prog,

classical and jazz and he returned in 1986. As for Mann, possibly because he was associated with the 1960s pop scene, in the 1970s, he never received his due recognition as a pioneering keyboardist in the same way that his contemporaries Keith Emerson, Rick Wakeman and Tony Banks did.

Although *Solar Fire* failed to chart in the UK, it climbed to number 96 on the Billboard chart in May 1974 thanks to regular live dates in the USA. It would be another three years before MMEB tasted major International success with *The Roaring Silence* album and breakthrough single 'Blinded by the Light' by which time Rogers had been replaced by singer Chris Thompson and guitarist Dave Flett.

The cover artwork for *Solar Fire* is no great shakes, featuring a starfield and bright lights, which continues on the back of the gatefold. The band's now-familiar circular logo first appeared on the 1972 *Glorified Magnified* album sleeve.

Side one
'Father of Day, Father of Night' 9:57 (Bob Dylan)

The band wastes no time in displaying their progressive rock credentials with this near ten-minute treatment of a song that closed Bob Dylan's *New Morning* album in 1970. A Dylan song featured on all three of the previous albums and in the 1960s, Manfred Mann plundered Dylan's songbook for several UK hits, including 'If You Gotta Go, Go Now', 'Just Like a Woman' and 'Mighty Quinn'. The original version of 'Father of Night' – Dylan's interpretation of the Jewish prayer 'Amidah' – lasts a little over a minute and a half, so clearly, this was going to be a radical reworking.

The haunting intro of ambient spacey sounds and choir is clearly influenced by György Ligeti's atonal contributions to the *2001: A Space Odyssey* soundtrack. At the one minute mark, the band comes crashing through the airlock with Mann's piano and Hammond leading the way. Haunting Mellotron strings underpin Mick Rogers' stately verses with his guitar soaring skywards for the chorus and bridge. It has an early King Crimson feel, especially Chris Slade's restrained drumming while Rogers' blistering solo at the halfway mark channels Jan Akkerman.

'Father of Day, Father of Night' is a stunning exercise in controlled power that erupts into instrumental flights of sheer joy. Unsurprisingly, it was performed on the 1973 tour and as a live favourite, with the band in existence to this day, it has endured.

'In the Beginning, Darkness' 5:25 (Manfred Mann, Mick Rogers, Chris Slade)

Opening with heavy fuzzed guitar chords, this has a funky psychedelic vibe that harks back to the 1960s. The rhythm loop from Slade's martial-like drumming and Pattenden's pumping bass line is inspired, and Mann indulges in some

Minimoog knob-twiddling to produce the rising pitch effects. It develops into a guitar-led jam before the return of Rogers' vocal melody with soulful backing and Slade's rapid-fire drumming.

Along with 'Joybringer', the band mimed to 'In the Beginning, Darkness' on the 1973 Swiss TV pop show *Hits A GoGo,* where the audience proved you could dance to it – providing you wore the requisite flared loon pants and tank top of course. Despite the easy-going vibe, it's an ambitious song that documents the creation and evolution of Earth and, although there are no religious references, the title and words have their origins in the book of Genesis 1:1-31.

'Pluto the Dog' 2:50 (Mann, Rogers, Slade, Colin Pattenden)

Although in a very different style, the album's first instrumental continues the mood and tempo of the previous track. The title is a light-hearted play on words – referencing both the dwarf planet of the solar system and Mickey Mouse's lovable companion. Pluto made his first appearance in a Walt Disney cartoon in 1930, the same year the planet was discovered.

A samba shuffle rhythm and incessant walking bass line provide a solid foundation for various percussive sounds – natural and courtesy of Minimoog – punctuated by sampled dog barks. It's topped off with an ear-piercing, fuzzed organ solo, but at under three minutes, it doesn't outstay its welcome, bringing side one to a playful close.

Side two
'Solar Fire' 5:18 (Slade, Rogers)

Wailing Minimoog launches the title song and side two of the LP. Enhanced by the female backing singers, it maintains the laid back groove of side one; clearly, the band had been listening to the Latin moods and rhythms of Santana.

'Solar Fire' refers to a powerful burst of intense energy and radiation on the sun's surface. The words of this title song are also an evocative description of the night sky turning into day – 'See the morning dancer, crossing the sky'.

Rogers' guitar fills have a bluesy edge and his discordant solo that dominates the song's second half cries and screams like a wailing banshee. Mann's Hammond embellishments and Slade and Pattenden's impeccable rhythm hold the whole thing together. Slade enjoyed a prolific career, drumming for the likes of Uriah Heep, the Firm, David Gilmour, AC/DC and Asia. When he and Pattenden left MMEB in the late 1970s, they reunited for the band Terra Nova before disbanding after one single and album.

According to certain internet sources, this song was written by the whole band but the label on the original LP credits Slade and Rogers as the sole authors.

'Saturn, Lord of the Ring / Mercury, The Winged Messenger'
6:36 (Mann / Mann, Rogers)

This is the album's second instrumental and as the title suggests, it's divided into two distinct parts. For the title of the first part, Mann alludes to both Saturn the planet, famous for its ringed system, and J.R.R. Tolkien's *The Lord of the Rings*, which was an essential read in the 1970s. Crashing cymbals and a moody guitar solo get things underway. Rogers' fiery salvos would make John McLaughlin proud while maintaining the melodic theme that gives the piece its lift. At 3:10, it comes to a sudden, momentary halt.

The second part takes its title – but not its music – from the third movement of Holst's *The Planets* suite, the original inspiration for the album. Discreet cymbal taps take up the cause and, along with a pulsing bassline, provides the rhythm for Mann's synth pyrotechnics. Around the 4:50 mark, it really gets into its proggy stride with stunning guitar and keyboard exchanges before chasing headlong to the finish line, ending with a bombastic flourish worthy of ELP.

'Joybringer' 3:25 (Gustav Holst, Mann, Rogers, Slade)

Although the tracklisting on the sleeve for the 1973 American release was the same as the UK version, the label on the LP told a different story. 'Joybringer' replaced 'Earth, the Circle Part 1' and 'Earth, The Circle Part 2' was moved to the end. It was a common ploy dating back to the early 1960s for American record labels to add hit singles to boost album sales and that was the case with 'Joybringer'. It was included as a bonus track on the 1998 reissue in all regions.

In addition to covering Dylan's songs, Mann was not averse to borrowing from the 20th-century classics and Holst's spirited melody was ideal for a prog rock interpretation. The mood is more exuberant and infectious than anything else on *Solar Fire* by some distance with a spirited blend of fuzzed guitar and Moog. The instrumental bridge in particular – to paraphrase the title – is a real joy. I couldn't resist buying the vinyl single back in 1973 and it's still tucked away somewhere in my record collection.

Released the previous year, 'Make Your Stash' by Daddy Cool included a similar sax-led treatment of Holst's tune, although the lyrics by Ross Wilson are decidedly more tongue-in-cheek.

'Earth, The Circle Part 2' 3:21 (Mann)

It's long been a mystery to me why 'Earth, The Circle Part 2' proceeds part one on the album, but the band – or perhaps the record label – must have had their reasons.

Part two opens with unaccompanied guitar before the punchy rhythm kicks in. Rogers sings the song's four solitary lines 'You hold the fire, You're where we lie' and 'You are the air, You hold our lives'. Short and sweet they may be, but the words are an affirming tribute to the planet on which we live. In contrast, the music and tone are brash and edgy.

The midsection is occupied by Mann's dissonant Hammond soloing, although the guitar and synth theme that follows is suitably triumphant. The jagged rhythms and sharp twists and turns bring early Gentle Giant to mind, and as you would expect, the whole thing is incredibly well played.

'Earth, The Circle Part 1' 3:57 (Claude Debussy, Mann)

The closing track opens with moody piano chords, accompanied by restrained Mellotron strings and Mann's pleasant, reverb-treated vocals. His lyrics elaborate on the theme of part two – celebrating the Earth as the sustainer of life. The mood is broken by jarring Moog punctuations, more typical of Keith Emerson than Mann. Although uncredited on the original LP, the delicate piano melody that follows is adapted from Debussy's 'Jimbo's Lullaby'. It's the second movement of his *Children's Corner* suite, published in 1908.

It changes course around the two-minute mark, joined by drums, bass, trombone and twangy guitar fills that develop into a mid-tempo jazz swing that disappointingly fades before reaching its full potential. It's perhaps not surprising that it was left off the original American LP release to make way for 'Joybringer'.

Electric Light Orchestra – *On the Third Day*

Personnel:
Jeff Lynne: vocals, guitars
Richard Tandy: Moog, piano, clavinet, Wurlitzer electric piano
Michael de Albuquerque: bass, backing vocals
Bev Bevan: drums, percussion
Mik Kaminski: violin on side one, excluding 'Showdown'
Mike Edwards: cello
Wilf Gibson: violin on 'Showdown' & side two
Colin Walker: cello on 'Showdown' & side two
Additional personnel:
Marc Bolan: lead guitar on 'Ma Ma Ma Belle' & 'Dreaming of 4000'
Produced at De Lane Lea Studios & AIR Studios, London by Jeff Lynne
Recording date: April to August 1973
UK release date: 14 December 1973, USA release date: November 1973
UK record label: Warner Bros., USA record label: United Artists
Highest chart places: UK: Did not chart, USA: 52, Canada: 40
Running time: 39:20

When multi-talented musicians Roy Wood and Jeff Lynne formed The Electric Light Orchestra in 1970, they had a succinct mission statement; to pick up from where The Beatles' *Magical Mystery Tour* left off. Due to their commitments with Birmingham pop-rockers the Move, the self-titled debut album didn't appear until December 1971. Released as a single the following summer, It was the lead song from the album '10538 Overture' that piqued the public's interest. It marked the beginning of a string of hit singles that lasted well into the 1980s. It's the quality and tenor of ELO's album material, however, that justifies their place in this book.

ELO 2 and *On the Third Day* were both released in 1973, which meant another head-scratching conundrum for the author. In the end, I went with the latter by virtue of the fact that it was their best produced and most concise recording to date. With the chart-friendly Wizzard and a solo career beckoning, Roy Wood left the band the previous year, leaving Jeff Lynne at the helm. He's supported by drummer and fellow ex-Move member Bev Bevan, the versatile and very talented keyboardist Richard Tandy, bassist Mike de Albuquerque and the all-important string section of Mik Kaminski, Mike Edwards, Wilf Gibson and Colin Walker. Partway through the sessions, violinist Kaminski replaced a departing Gibson and Walker soon followed.

With Roy Wood out of the frame, Lynne is the sole songwriter. He convincingly forges art rock and progressive pop with classical influences into a crafted sound that would reach its peak in 1977 with the *Out of the Blue* album. With the exception of 'In the Hall of the Mountain King', Lynne would be responsible for all the band's material for the duration of the 1970s.

Due to their popularity and chart success in North America, ELO crossed the Atlantic several times in 1973, supporting the likes of Jethro Tull before headlining later in the year. A typical setlist in December featured the entire album – minus 'Dreaming of 4000' – along with crowd-pleasers '10538 Overture', 'Great Balls of Fire' and 'Roll Over Beethoven'.

The album cover features Lynne's visage visible through a cut-out section above the crescent of planet Earth. It may well have been inspired by the sequence in Stanley Kubrick's 1968 sci-fi epic *2001: A Space Odyssey* where the Star Child looks down on Earth. It's an improvement on the American cover, which features a black and white group photograph with the band exposing their navels. Hugh McDowell appears in the photo and although he doesn't play on the album, he had a long association with ELO.

Side one
'Ocean Breakup / King of the Universe' 4:05 (Jeff Lynne)
The band's classical aspirations are evident from the start with a strident orchestral intro similar to Andrew Lloyd Webber's theme for *Phantom of the Opera*. The morse code-like rhythmic pulses foreshadow Roger Waters' song 'The Tide Is Turning (After Live Aid)' by some fourteen years. Underlining the band's remit, the string arrangement is straight out of 'I Am the Walrus', sounding vibrant and fulsome with plenty of bottom end from the cello.

Sweet strings are followed by a Moog and staccato rhythm fanfare that herald the haunting vocal melody. Lynne's wordless crooning brings The Beach Boys to mind, gradually developing into the verses and stately chorus. The words are few but contradictory where the protagonist is both fearful – 'I am so afraid' and bold – 'I am King, King of the Sky' before the song draws to a calming conclusion.

'Bluebird Is Dead' 4:25 (Lynne)
Taken at a languid pace with a walking bass line, this melancholic tune is anything but pedestrian. The Beatles influence is ever-present with Lynne's measured vocal releasing his inner John Lennon, punctuated by mournful descending strings. The chugging chorus ups the tempo a shade as Lynne, singing in the first person, finds it hard to accept that a loving relationship has turned sour, with bluebird being a metaphor for his love. The middle-eight strays into honky-tonk territory with a 4/4 rhythm and a searing, heavily processed guitar solo.

'Bluebird Is Dead' has a similar feel to 'Blackbird' on The Beatles' *The White Album* and 'Bluebird' on Paul McCartney & Wings' *Band on the Run*. McCartney penned both songs and typically, they have a more wistful and optimistic tone.

'Oh No Not Susan' 3:27 (Lynne)
Following a mellow intro led by Albuquerque's throbbing bassline, the third track takes off with a frenetic instrumental sequence that almost morphs into

Mason Williams' 'Classical Gas'. It's the song's best part with distinct proggy overtones. It soon settles into a plodding groove with Mik Kaminski's violin weaving snake-like around Lynne's brooding vocal where once again the ghost of John Lennon is ever-present.

The titular Susan is an aristocrat who hobnobs with 'lords and dukes' but ultimately rejects her privileged lifestyle because, as the chorus would have it, 'They just don't mean a fucking thing'. Somehow this line managed to evade the scrutiny of the BBC, who deemed the song fit for radio consumption. The chorus is certainly memorable, supported by strings swaying back and forth. At 2:54, Tandy's synth takes over, followed by a lively reprise of the intro to bring the song full circle.

In the UK, 'Oh No Not Susan' was the B side to the single release of 'Ma-Ma-Ma Belle'. It remains a curious subject for a song, particularly given the social and economic hardships that many endured in 1973.

'New World Rising / Ocean Breakup (Reprise)' 4:40 (Lynne)

Side one of *On the Third Day* was originally intended as a suite with four interlinking songs, which explains why the opening piece returns for the climax here. A pulsating synth line – later to be replaced by violin – underpins Lynne's treated vocal before he reverts to his normal tone for the second verse. 'New World Rising' is a celebration of life, embracing each new day with breezy optimism – 'Hey, Good mornin', how you doin', well I'm doin' fine'.

Bevan's explosive drum fills are complemented by swirling strings which accelerate like a runaway train as synth takes the lead for the expansive instrumental section. It's an absolute joy and would be further developed as 'Fire on High', the epic opener to ELO's fifth studio album, *Face the Music,* two years later. Kaminski's violin solo provides a brief classical-inspired respite, and at 3:35, it morphs into the brooding climax of 'Ocean Breakup' with crashing chords providing a powerful finale to side one of the original UK vinyl release.

'Showdown' 4:15 (Lynne)

As with Manfred Mann's Earth Band's 'Joybringer', I've transgressed my own rules here by including a song that appeared on the original LP in America but not in the UK. After the pomp and drama of the previous track, 'Showdown' is a song you can actually dance to – and we did in 1973. It's Tandy's incessant clavinet that gives it that funky edge and Gibson and Walker recreate the Philadelphia string sound that in 1973 swept the airwaves and discotheques – that's a nightclub for those of you too young to remember.

This is another song about a relationship that's heading for a fall, or more precisely, a 'Showdown'. When it was released as a single, it reached No 12 in the UK in November 1973 and 53 on the American Billboard chart. It also did well in parts of mainland Europe. With its catchy choral hook and infectious rhythm, 'Showdown' has endured and was used to good effect for a memorable bowling scene in the 1996 comedy film *Kingpin.*

Side Two
'Daybreaker' 3:50 (Lynne)

This is a glorious instrumental to set side two in motion. From the opening bars, it has an expansive feel, combining classical influences with pop sensibilities to good effect. It romps along at a brisk pace with synth arpeggios underscored by playful strings, a joyful rhythm pattern and an earworm of a tune. Unsurprisingly, it opened the band's setlist on the subsequent tour and is the lead track on the 1974 live album *The Night the Light Went On in Long Beach*. It remained a stage favourite for some years to come.

'Daybreaker' was the B side of the 'Ma-Ma-Ma Belle' single released in America in February the following year and proved to be more popular than the A-side, although it only reached 87 in the Billboard chart. It did a little better across the border, peaking at 57 in Canada. It remains my favourite track on the album.

'Ma-Ma-Ma Belle' 3:52 (Lynne)

From the sublime to the ridiculous, you might say, but that's not intended as a put-down. Lynne's friend and high profile glam rocker Marc Bolan makes an uncredited appearance as joint lead guitarist and if I'm not mistaken, the heavy riffing intro is his handiwork. This is a rock and roll blast with a rock solid rhythm section and rhythmic string embellishments sounding equally at home. Lynne is clearly a rock and roller at heart, belting out the repeated choral refrain in the style of Little Richard and all the other 1950s pioneers.

The song's protagonist is a man obsessed with who wants to possess his 'Ma Belle' (My Beautiful), although the lyrics were clearly designed to fit the mood rather than tell a story. When 'Ma-Ma-Ma Belle' was released as a single in the UK, it stalled at number 22 in April 1974, failing to crack the top 20 as the previous three singles had done.

'Dreaming of 4000' 5:00 (Lynne)

The penultimate song is more in keeping with the tracks on side one, balancing a memorable chorus with adventurous instrumental breaks. A synth fanfare, spacey effects and a twangy guitar break – Bolan again? – give way to a surging, mid-tempo song supported by strummed acoustic guitar, Moog and shimmering strings. The lyrical middle-eight is probably the best part, especially the cascading strings, and the instrumental bridge is intoxicating.

The lyrics are ambiguous and open to several interpretations including religion: 'And the lord of life came following, his sins to be forgiven', impending doom 'Take heed of the warnin' or you know it's gonna be too late' and blurring dreams with reality 'My world is saved and I am free, but in the night, still I know I must be dreaming'. The relevance of '4000' in the title – which isn't referenced in the lyrics – remains elusive.

'In the Hall of the Mountain King' 6:35 (Edvard Grieg)

To close the album, a cover of one of the most popular works in the classical repertoire. It pre-empts Rick Wakeman's interpretation of the same piece in *Journey to the Centre of the Earth* the following year. The track actually begins with Tandy's delicate keyboard rendition of the pastoral and equally famous 'Morning Mood', which is also taken from Grieg's 'Peer Gynt Suite No. 1'.

Ominous strings follow, with Tandy's keys providing the percussive effects before Bevan's explosive drum volley brings the piece to life. With cellos and drums cranked to the maximum, it lurches at a breakneck pace all the way to the bombastic finale. Along the way, Gibson's stunning Gypsy-like violin solo threatens to take over the piece, almost turning it into a lively reel before returning to Grieg's malevolent theme. This was another stage favourite and closed the main set during the *On the Third Day* tour.

Magma – *Mekanïk Destruktïẁ Kommandöh*
Personnel:
Klaus Blasquiz: vocals, percussion
Stella Vander: vocals
Muriel Streisfield: vocals
Evelyne Razymovski: vocals
Michele Saulnier: vocals
Doris Reinhardt: vocals
René Garber: bass clarinet, vocals
Teddy Lasry: brass, flute
Jean-Luc Manderlier: piano, organ
Claude Olmos: guitar
Jannick Top: bass
Christian Vander: drums, vocals, organ, percussion
Produced at Manor Studios, England & Aquarium Studios, Paris by Giorgio
Gomelsky
Recording date: April 1973
Release date: December 1973
Record label: A&M
Highest chart places: UK: Did not chart, USA: Did not chart, France: Did not chart
Running time: 38:47

Like several of their contemporaries on the opposite side of the German
border, the rock mainstream was the anathema to French collective Magma
and visionary bandleader, songwriter Christian Vander. Their third studio
outing *Mekanïk Destruktïẁ Kommandöh* (or *MDK* for short) is a concept that's
ambitious in scope and execution. It's the third part of a story set in the distant
future that has social-political, ecological and spiritual overtones and although
on the surface, there are parallels with Gong's *Radio Gnome Invisible Trilogy*,
Vander's vision is a darker, more serious affair.

The story began in 1970 on Magma's eponymous debut album where a
group of people, fearful of Earth's self-destructive tendencies, journey to
the fictional planet Kobaïa where they settle. On the second album, *1001°
Centigrades* (1971), a party of colonists return to Earth to spread a message of
spiritual enlightenment but come into conflict with the authorities.Following
their return to Kobaïa, an Earth-based spiritualist named Nebëhr Gudahtt is the
principal subject of *MDK*.

Not content with either French or English – or any other known language
for that matter – Vander invented a whole new dialect for the song lyrics
which he dubbed 'Kobaïan'. He was following in the footsteps of J.R.R.
Tolkien, who created Elvish for *The Lord of the Rings* and Marc Okrand, who
was responsible for the Klingons' guttural speech in *Star Trek*. Kobaïan is
a kind of French / German / Russian hybrid that developed from the songs
themselves. The words aside, musically, Vander was heavily influenced by

John Coltrane, which he combines with classical influences including Carl Orff and Stravinsky. Throw Frank Zappa, Béla Bartók and Stockhausen into the mix and you have a heady brew.

When interviewed in 2015, Vander stated: 'Progressive rock is a term that means nothing to me. It does not define the music of Magma in any way'.

In much the same way as bands tagged 'Canterbury', 'Krautrock' or even 'symphonic', he was wary of labels and devised his own term 'Zeuhl' for the band's idiosyncratic musical style. The term achieved cult status and is synonymous with bands that followed in Magma's musical footsteps. Vander explained: 'Zeuhl is a sound. When you say it, it is like a vibration. It represents the interior speed and the rhythmic division of the music'.

Vander wrote the album comparatively quickly and unusually, the story evolved from the songs rather than the other way round. The recording process, however was a protracted one, involving changes in studios and sound engineers. This led to mistakes, but despite all this, Vander has fond memories of the period. Prior to the recording, he completely revamped the line-up with only himself, vocalist Klaus Blasquiz and wind instrumentalist Teddy Lasry remaining from the previous album.

On the album cover, the distinctive Magma symbol makes its second appearance and would feature on later releases as well as their stage backdrop with the band all conspicuously dressed in black. On the back is the heading 'Third movement of Theusz Hamtaahk'. Originally Theusz Hamtaahk – which translates into English as 'Time of the Hatred' – was intended to consist of nine movements but was abandoned for practical reasons.

Side one
'Hortz Fur Dëhn Stekëhn West' 9:34 (Christian Vander)

Despite the individual track listings, *MDK* is not so much a suite as it is a continuous work separated on two sides of vinyl. The lyrics printed inside the LP sleeve are in Kobaïan, so any attempts to decipher the narrative are fruitless. Suffice to say, the story involves a spiritualist named Nebëhr Gudahtt, who takes up the Kobaians' cause following their visit to Earth. He attempts to convince the people of earth that their only salvation from impending disaster is purification and communication with 'The Spirit of the Universe' – Kreühn Köhrmahn. At first, his message is rejected and the people rise up against him. Gradually, they begin to understand and accept his wisdom and join his cause.

This is by far the longest track and sets the tone for the rest of the album. It begins with a jangly repeated piano chord progression joined by chant-like male voices that are half-sung, half-spoken. Despite the unfamiliar language, the tone is very Teutonic, almost aggressive. At 2:19, a loud drone appears out of nowhere that's both unsettling and hypnotic. The vocals and brass become fuller and more intense, with operatic female voices joining the fray.

Prominent guitar enters at 4:10, playing the skeleton of a melody, but the opening rhythm pattern remains constant throughout. At 6:30, the massed choir reaches a powerful crescendo with organ providing instrumental support. Vander and his team have not finished yet; the tempo becomes even more urgent with staccato chords, percussion and vocal punctuations. Around the eight-minute mark, the dense arrangement has a cinematic quality before male voices rush headlong to the finish. An assault to the senses, it leaves the listener dazed and it's only the opening track.

'Ïma Süri Dondaï' 4:28 (Vander)

Track two builds upon the foundation laid by the opening song with a relentless stop-start rhythm and clashing male and female vocals. It's all very melodramatic and again, the combination of strident horns and choral chanting is powerfully effective. Female voices take the lead, backed by an urgent jazz-rock theme featuring guitar and sax. The counterpoint voices are mesmerising, weaving in and out of each other to dizzying effect. It reaches a stirring climax that would do justice to a Hollywood biblical epic from the 1950s.

Even though there are only eight singers credited on the album – including Vander himself – the vocals dominate the arrangements, often acting as another instrument, both melodically and rhythmically.

'Kobaïa Iss Dëh Hündïn' 3:35 (Vander)

The final track on side one features Jean-Luc Manderlier's rhythmic piano motif. It builds in tempo, joined by voices, Claude Olmos' inventive guitar and Christian Vander's clattering drums. It maintains the same groove with screeching brass stabs before the voices chant a martial-like rhythm that reaches a fever pitch before subsiding. The piano rhythm continues undaunted with random guitar and organ embellishments before fading to make way for side two.

Side two
'Da Zeuhl Wortz Mëkanïk' 7:48 (Vander)

A mantra-like chant opens side two, accompanied by Vander and Jannick Top's infectious rhythm pattern before fading to a whisper. A jazz-rock sequence follows with another imaginative vocal arrangement where the prominent female choir is joined by a guitar doubling the vocal melody. Gradually, Stella Vander's soprano rises to the fore, singing the impossibly high notes in a different key to disorientating effect. So far, so engaging, but her singing becomes more erratic – and to the listener more challenging – while the backing maintains the metronomic rhythm accompanied by improvised jazz guitar.

Around the six-minute mark, it reaches a crescendo before continuing at a less frantic but still purposeful tempo. Vander throws in some inventive drum fills before the voices accelerate to a finale that has the majesty of a Wagnerian opera.

MDK is regularly compared with Carl Orff's 'O Fortuna' from the *Carmina Burana* cantata and there are certainly similarities in the strident choral arrangements. Vander's work, however, is less elaborate, with a greater reliance on repetition. The individual singing is also less disciplined and intentionally so, conveying the discord and turmoil of Vander's future world.

'Nebëhr Gudahtt' 6:00 (Vander)

This song is named after the prophet Nebëhr Gudahtt who's central to the story. It begins with subdued piano repeating the vocal melody from the previous song, overlaid with decorative guitar lines. It continues at a hesitant pace with a solo soprano, random bass notes and percussion, while piano repeats the rhythmic arpeggios. The female soloist becomes more frenzied, contrasting with a harsh, guttural male vocal while Vander's tuned percussion provides the sweetener.

At this point, *MDK* reaches its most intense and challenging moment with the female soloist literally screaming out the words. The backing continues to build in tempo with biting guitar notes that develop into a cacophonic frenzy before strident brass arrives to take over proceedings and lead everyone to the abrupt conclusion.

'Nebëhr Gudahtt' has proven to be one of the album's most enduring songs, becoming a perennial stage favourite. At the time of writing – October 2021 – Magma are in the midst of a European tour with Christian Vander still at the helm and Stella Vander on vocals. Given that drumming has taken its toll on the likes of Nick Mason, Alan White and Phil Collins, it's to Vander's credit that he's still hammering the skins at the age of 74.

'Mëkanïk Kömmandöh' 4:08 (Vander)

The penultimate song follows the now-familiar pattern with a shuffle rhythm driven by drums, bass and improvised guitar chords. The strident choral chanting is doubled by brass to arresting effect and once again, the counterpoint vocal arrangements are superb. At the halfway mark, it accelerates at a rapid rate, led by horns with the male and female singers exchanging separate vocal lines. Following a bluesy, impromptu guitar break, it goes into overdrive, reaching a tense climax before release comes in the shape of an arousing finale.

'Kreühn Köhrmahn Ïss Dëh Hündin' 3:14 (Vander)

Once again, piano sets the wheels in motion with a sparse melody, joined by massed female voices and a stately rhythm. Similar to the 'Nebëhr Gudahtt' track, the female lead singer works herself into an overwrought frenzy. At the halfway mark, the drum pattern takes on a funeral march-like dirge joined by menacingly loud horns. Anyone listening to the album on headphones would be wise to take them off at this point before it comes to a dead stop, leaving a suspended, high pitched note to close. It's an unconventional ending to a very unconventional album.

MDK remained in Magma's repertoire throughout the 1970s and was performed on their first American tour in 1973. Their best-known work, it has overshadowed much of their other output and has been released and reissued in several variations over the years. It's not everyone's cup of prog, however, and remains one of the most divisive albums of 1973.

Yes – *Tales from Topographic Oceans*

Personnel:
Jon Anderson: lead vocals, acoustic guitar, percussion
Steve Howe: guitars, electric sitar, backing vocals
Chris Squire: bass guitar, backing vocals
Rick Wakeman: keyboards
Alan White: drums, percussion, backing vocals
Produced at Morgan Studios, London by Yes & Eddie Offord
Recording date: May – October 1973
Release date: 7 December 1973
Record label: Atlantic
Highest chart places: UK: 1, USA: 6, Canada: 4
Running time: 81:14

Referring to *Tales from Topographic Oceans* in 2007, *Prog Rock* magazine made the bold statement 'You either love it or hate it'. I'm not so sure; there's a school of thought that it would have made a very fine single LP. For me, at just over 81 minutes, it's fine as it is. Some, however, found it difficult to digest on its initial release, particularly critics who had review deadlines to meet. Earlier in the year, Yes had also swept the board in the *Melody Maker* annual poll, so a backlash was perhaps inevitable.

When Yes entered the studio in May 1973, It was on the back of their most prestigious tour to date promoting *Close to the Edge*, considered by many to be the definitive progressive rock album, so they had a tough act to follow. They had also survived the unthinkable, the loss of drummer Bill Bruford, replaced by the equally talented Alan White. It was perhaps for the best; Bruford is an exceptional drummer, but I doubt that *Topographic Oceans* would have appealed to his jazz sensibilities, being, for the most part, symphonic rock.

By 1973, singer Jon Anderson had asserted himself as the band's leader and visionary. Although he wasn't a musician himself – not yet anyway – he was surrounded by four of the best and with each subsequent album, he set his sights higher. Having composed with bassist Chris Squire on the earlier albums, he had an ally in guitarist Steve Howe who was equally ambitious. *The Yes Album*, *Fragile* and *Close to the Edge* had all raised the bar, so a double concept album seemed like a natural progression. It was certainly a mouth-watering prospect for fans.

While Rick Wakeman had been motivated by *The Private Life of Henry VIII*, Anderson's inspiration came from a more spiritual literary source, Paramahansa Yogananda's *Autobiography of a Yogi*, or more specifically, the detailed footnote. The four-part Shastric scriptures described by Yogananda set the wheels in motion for a four-sided epic which Anderson developed with Howe over the coming months while Yes were on tour. They met initial resistance when the composition was presented to the rest of the band and, while Squire and the others were unsure of their parts at times, they all pitched in to make the album a success.

The arduous recording of *Topographic Oceans* has been exhaustively documented elsewhere – wooden cows et al – which I won't dwell upon here – but suffice to say, the band's dedication and the heroic work of producer Eddie Offord ensured the whole complex process came to a fruitful end. Sonically, it was their best-recorded album to date. The subsequent tour rolled into action on 16 November 1973, but the band's troubles were not over yet.

Similar to the *A Passion Play* scenario five months earlier, critics, including *Melody Maker* writer Chris Welch, poured scorn on the shows and album. Fans, however, by and large, took a different view and responded with their pockets and feet. As discussed earlier, my friends and I were knocked out by the *Topographic Oceans* shows, which, like a fine wine, matured with each successive performance, enhanced by Roger Dean's stunning stage design. Many fans must have received a record token in their Christmas stocking because while the rest of the nation was toasting in the New Year, Yes celebrated *Topographic Oceans* reaching the top of the UK album chart.

Although the cover artwork is probably Dean's most iconic, for me, it doesn't quite match the splendour of the waterfall painting for *Close to the Edge*. The images suggested by Anderson and White seem out of place in the overall landscape. At the time, I mused that the five fishes on the back of the gatefold represented the band members, with one fish – clearly a different species – being Rick Wakeman. I'm only speculating, of course.

Side one
'The Revealing Science of God – Dance of the Dawn' 20:27
(Jon Anderson, Steve Howe, Chris Squire, Rick Wakeman, Alan White)
When interviewed by Chris Welch for *Melody Maker* in 1973, Anderson predicted, 'People who didn't get on with *Close to the Edge* won't like this one either, unless they are prepared to sacrifice some time to get into it'. Certainly, if they found the twittering birds and rippling water that opened the previous album perplexing, then Anderson's hymnal, mantra-like chant that begins here would have been equally bewildering. A two-minute, ambient instrumental intro was also recorded – as featured on the 2003 reissue – but was removed for the original LP release.

As the chanting develops, it's overwhelmed by White's snare volley and Wakeman's synth fanfare. In the first of three main sections, guitar followed by Minimoog play a jaunty tune in 6/8 with a quasi-calypso rhythm and Howe plays his trusty Gibson ES-175 high on the neck. The harmonised vocals are rich and fulsome and the spiralling 'Moment, moment, moment' hook individually sung by Squire, Howe and Anderson in succession is glorious. At 6:54, it moves up several gears with Howe's snarling guitar and White's shuffle tom-tom rhythm locking superbly. A moment of quiet reflection features harmonious guitar with delicate bass fills and ascending Mellotron strings.

Interviewed in 1992, Howe reflected that he and Anderson had written the song about events that were personal to them – 'what happened to this song we once knew so well'. The words have a universal resonance with evolution, ecological and anti-war themes in the verses and an underlying message that young people hold the key to the future – 'Move over glory to sons of old fighters past'. Anderson later regretted the reference to God in the title, feeling that the religious connotations may have been an unintended distraction for some.

Following a sudden surge in tempo at 11.10, Anderson's word couplet 'Skyline teacher, Warland seeker' is a throwback to the abstract wordplay of 'Siberian Khatru'. It leads into an instrumental sequence with contrasting guitar solos supported by prominent bass and drums and synth, piano and Mellotron embellishments. A mellow electric sitar interlude welcomes Anderson back, building to a powerful 'La, La, La' choral chant. A scorching Moog solo at 16:50 is one of Wakeman's finest, crackling with energy with Squire and White spurring him on. The triumphant vocal melody that concludes is a throwback to the similarly grandiose finale to 'Close to the Edge'.

'The Revealing Science of God' was deservedly resurrected in later years and featured on *Keys to Ascension* (October 1996) and *Topographic Drama – Live Across America* (November 2017). It was also enthusiastically performed on the 2002 American tour by the reformed 1973 line-up with Wakeman clearly at peace with the work.

Side two
'The Remembering – High the Memory' 20:38 (Anderson, Howe, Squire, Wakeman, White)

In 1974, Anderson said of 'The Remembering': 'We try to recall our lives and in so doing, get the listener to recall his. It's best described as a calm sea of music'. In 1992, Howe was more succinct, describing it as 'A much lighter, folky side of Yes'. Both descriptions are apt; it's the album's most placid offering, combining folksy song elements with quasi-classical, instrumental interludes. Overall, its reflective charms are a perfect foil to the complexity and drama of sides one and three.

It begins with a wistful Moog and electric sitar theme. In keeping with Anderson's description, there's a nautical thread that runs through the dream-like opening section with references to 'sails afloat', 'velvet sailors' and 'course the compass' in the verses and 'Sail away among your dreams' in the chorus. The lyrics are a pointer to the next album *Relayer*, and the opening line in the equally pastoral 'To Be Over'.

The symphonic Moog and Mellotron arrangement hinted at 4:35 before blossoming at 7:35 is one of the highpoints of *Topographic Oceans*. Hauntingly romantic, it's the album's answer to the soaring 'Eclipse' theme in 'And You and I'. One would have anticipated Wakeman to be responsible for writing this sequence, but just as Bill Bruford had a hand in 'Eclipse', White claimed the credit in 1974. Wakeman was preoccupied for a good deal of 1973, working on his own masterwork *Journey to the Centre of the Earth*, which was unveiled the following January.

In the second section, Anderson's upbeat delivery is accompanied by Howe's lively twelve-string guitar. The urgent electric sequence that follows is glued together by Squire's stunning fretless bass playing, which he remained justly proud of. The word 'Relayer' begins each line of the chorus, providing another link to *Topographic Oceans*' successor released the following year. Following a brief reprise of the symphonic sequence, Anderson is accompanied by lute, Mellotron flute and organ.

The final section returns to the themes established earlier, only with a greater sense of urgency where the bass is again at the heart of the elaborate chord sequence. A haunting instrumental section featuring Moog, Mellotron, cymbal washes and weeping guitar evoke a sense of anticipation and the band duly deliver. At 18:30, Howe's guitar phrase and the soaring keys from the 'What happened to this song' finale on side one are reprised before Anderson leads the band to an uplifting conclusion.

At the end of February 1974, during the American leg of the *Topographic Oceans* tour, 'The Remembering' was dropped in favour of more familiar material. It has remained absent from the band's setlist ever since and failed to materialise during the 2016 and 2017 American tours when *Topographic Oceans* sides one and four were performed in their entirety along with part of side three.

Side three
'The Ancient – Giants Under the Sun' 18:34 (Anderson, Howe, Squire, Wakeman, White)

The shortest of the four sides of music, 'The Ancient', is also the most experimental and challenging. In 1974 Anderson explained, 'It's all about the ancients: civilisations like the Incas, the Mayas and Atlantis'. Although he's mixing the authentic with myth, the band's interpretation of the sound and atmosphere of indigenous, ethnic music using modern technology mostly pays off, successfully conjuring up images of abandoned temples and tropical jungles.

Howe and White are at the heart and soul of 'The Ancient' with guitar acting as a kind of traveller through the turbulent landscape. It opens with a gong resonating and splashing hi-hats, followed by a muscular drum loop, frantic vibraphone and bass underpinning piercing steel guitar. Out of this rhythmic discord, a melody gradually evolves on a soft cushion of strings. Stabbing chords punctuate Anderson's harmonised vocals, followed by a gorgeous Moog and Mellotron theme.

At 6:07, it sails into a delightful guitar-driven groove, providing the foundation for Anderson's chanted references to the 'Sun' in several languages. These include the Spanish 'Sol', the Greek 'Ilios', 'Dhoop' – the Hindi word for 'Sunshine', 'Ah Kin' which is Mayan for 'He of the Sun', and 'Saule', a traditional Lithuanian name meaning 'Sun'. The Mellotron strings – with a hint of choir – are an utter delight.

137

At 8:24, it comes to an abrupt stop, followed by four minutes of Yes at their most dissonant and demanding. Percussion and strings contrast with primaeval, reverberated guitar. White's drumming is both deft and economical and Howe cuts loose with a lengthy, improvised solo that screams and howls. It was a challenge to perform live and had to be modified slightly because of the tricky stops and starts.

At 12:20, the mayhem subsides and the listener's staying power is rewarded with the album's most accessible song. In a traditional verse-chorus format, 'Leaves of Green' is beautifully effective, even more so due to the discord that has preceded it. Anderson's words are a eulogy to lost civilisations, destroyed by powerful sources that claimed to be acting in the name of God. It features an extended classical guitar solo and is a rare instance where Howe's solo acoustic playing is incorporated into a Yes song.

Howe later performed the 'Leaves of Green' solo on stage as an alternative to the perennials 'Clap' and 'Mood for a Day'. As a standalone song, it features on *Topographic Drama – Live Across America* and *Yes 50 Live* (August 2019), with Jon Davison providing the vocals.

Side four
'Ritual – Nous Sommes du Soleil' 21:35 (Anderson, Howe, Squire, Wakeman, White)

Wisely, Yes saved the best till last. In 1974, Anderson described 'Ritual' as 'A love song, something very personal' although its appeal is again universal, resonating with an energy that's uplifting and empowering.

Squire's reverberating bass, punctuated by staccato chords, provides the atmospheric intro, and underpins Howe's Les Paul laying down the main theme. A second melody follows and gallops along at a jaunty pace with syncopated rhythms supporting Anderson's wordless harmonies. It's ridiculously infectious, especially when synth doubles the vocals. A rasping bass solo gives way to a moment of tranquillity where solo guitar recapitulates several of the album's themes, incorporating a snippet of 'Close to the Edge'. It flows into the romantic song 'Nous Sommes du Soleil' – 'We are of the sun' – with strings and choral backing.

Electric sitar provides sympathetic support for the secondary melody as Anderson intones 'Life seems like a fight' which was written by Howe, reflecting his personal feelings at the time. It builds to a majestic peak with the soaring 'At all' line repeated no less than eleven times. At 11.08, another tranquil interlude features bass front and centre, with a light dusting of percussion and keys. At the twelve-minute mark, Squire breaks into a sprint with his rampaging bass solo closely pursued by White's frantic drum pattern. Howe takes up the baton with a mesmerising solo, crossing the finish line at 14:19.

A dramatic percussive sequence follows, representing the conflict between love and hate. It was a real showstopper when performed live with White's furious solo accompanied by Anderson on percussion and Squire clearly enjoying himself hammering the kettle drums. Throughout, Roger Dean's animated drum riser spewed lights around the auditorium. White's drumming is particularly inventive, conveying the melody while Wakeman's shrilling synth effects pour on the heat.

At 16:55, a stately solo guitar theme heralds a moment of calm and serenity – love has triumphed. There is a sense of closure and coming to a journey's end – 'flying home, going home'. Electric and acoustic guitar, piano and organ complement Anderson's yearning reprise of 'Nous Sommes du Soleil'. The piano part was written by White and later embellished by Wakeman. Bass, drums and strings enter at 19:56 to bring the song and the album to a moving finale.

'Ritual' has enjoyed the most staying power as a stage song and has featured on several live albums. *Yesshows* (November 1980) features an extended version from 1976 and there's a particularly splendid version on *Symphonic Live* recorded in November 2001 and released on CD, DVD and Blu-ray. It also closed the main part of the set during the 35th Anniversary tour in 2004 with a rejuvenated Wakeman on keyboards.

Epilogue

After 1973, the fortunes of progressive rock acts in the 1970s varied. Unable to sustain their earlier success in a changing musical climate, the career of many bands such as Focus ended before the decade did. Others went from strength to strength as Supertramp's *Crime of the Century* (1974), Pink Floyd's *Wish You Were Here* (1975), Genesis' *A Trick of the Tail* (1976), Yes' *Going for the One* (1977) and Jethro Tull's *Heavy Horses* (1978) testify. Artistically, if not always commercially, a newer, diverse breed of acts like Journey, The Enid, The Alan Parsons Project, Anthony Phillips, Toto, National Health and Sweden's Kaipa also flourished in the late 1970s. Like Ant Phillips, two other ex-Genesis members, Peter Gabriel and Steve Hackett, embarked on prestigious solo careers that continue to this day.

In 1977, many acts were branded as dinosaurs by trend-hopping journalists, but it's a myth perpetuated by the media that prog was killed off by punk rock and new wave. Pink Floyd closed the decade with the hugely successful *The Wall*, Jethro Tull maintained a prestigious output and Yes went on to release their best selling album and single in 1983. Featuring ex-members of Yes, ELP, King Crimson and Genesis, 'supergroups' Asia and GTR fused prog with AOR and also charted highly, especially in the USA. Some bands faded altogether, only to re-emerge in later years, while others, including Barclay James Harvest, Renaissance and Camel, remodelled themselves and adopted a 1980s pop-rock style. Although popularity was not sustained, it was evident that the prog pioneers were not ready to give up just yet. King Crimson, for example, maintained their uncompromising prog rock stance with a trio of albums that began with *Discipline* (1981).

Just as importantly, a fresh breed of young upstarts sprung up in the 1980s under the so-called new wave banner of progressive rock, later dubbed neo-prog. Bands like Marillion, Twelfth Night, IQ, Galahad and Pendragon took their influences from Genesis and Pink Floyd in particular. Marillion frontman Fish confirmed as recently as 2021 that he was inspired by *Selling England by the Pound* and in 1985, Marillion's concept album *Misplaced Childhood* topped the UK chart. The following year, Genesis and Peter Gabriel released their best selling albums *Invincible Touch* and *So*, respectively, although the more progressive elements were tempered by a radio-friendly sheen.

In the 1990s, another revival saw a particularly strong showing of new acts from America and Scandinavia. At the forefront, Spock's Beard and The Flower Kings merged the musicality and complexity of 1970's Yes and Gentle Giant. In the UK, Mostly Autumn kept the progressive folk banner flying while internationally, bands like Arena, Echolyn, Änglagård and Pain of Salvation gave prog a fresh new makeover. Often fronted by a female singer, symphonic metal is a prog crossover genre that really found its feet in the late 1990s, with Finnish band Nightwish proving to be particularly popular. Pink Floyd, Genesis, Yes, Emerson, Lake & Palmer, Jethro Tull and King Crimson continued to release albums during the 1990s with varying degrees of commercial and artistic success.

Transatlantic were the first prog 'supergroup' of the new millennium and their Yes-inspired symphonic bombast is especially popular in mainland Europe. Like Transatlantic, Magenta formed in 1999 fronted by Christina Booth, while Rob Reed, the band's creative force, has more recently released several solo works indebted to Mike Oldfield. The eclectic 2003 debut album by The Tangent received a good deal of acclaim, referencing Yes, ELP and the Canterbury scene. Although Dream Theater have been around since 1985, spearheading progressive metal, their fortunes – commercially and artistically – took an upturn following the turn of the millennium. At the other end of the prog spectrum, Big Big Train, following a slow start, established themselves as one of the most respected and talented acts of the last two decades.

Several bands have found even greater success in the 21st century, including Porcupine Tree, fronted by the multi-talented Steven Wilson. Like Wilson, Tool have a penchant for Pink Floyd and King Crimson and along with Radiohead and Muse, they have returned prog and art rock to the stadiums and arenas previously filled by the likes of Pink Floyd and Emerson, Lake & Palmer. Although these bands may not necessarily appreciate the prog rock connection, they would certainly consider their music progressive in the truest sense of the word.

They are also the successful tip of a very large iceberg. Partly due to the advent of home recording technology, there have been more progressive rock albums released in the last two decades than at any other time in the genre's history. Many convey a nostalgic sense of deja vu, evidence of the music's enduring appeal, while others embody the same experimental and adventurous spirit that made 1973 one of the most fertile periods in the history of rock.

The story doesn't end there, however. Many bands that fell by the wayside in the late 1970s, such as Van der Graaf Generator, Focus and Curved Air, have enjoyed a new lease of life in the 21st century and continue touring and, or releasing albums to this day. Some, on the other hand, never went away. As I put the finishing touches to this book, on my to-do list for the *DPRP* are brand new albums from Yes, PFM and a Genesis tribute to review. As the late Greg Lake sang in 1973, it's 'the show that never ends'.

Also available from Sonicbond ...

On Track series

Tori Amos – Lisa Torem 978-1-78952-142-9
Asia – Peter Braidis 978-1-78952-099-6
Barclay James Harvest – Keith and Monica Domone 978-1-78952-067-5
The Beatles – Andrew Wild 978-1-78952-009-5
The Beatles Solo 1969-1980 – Andrew Wild 978-1-78952-030-9
Blue Oyster Cult – Jacob Holm-Lupo 978-1-78952-007-1
Marc Bolan and T.Rex – Peter Gallagher 978-1-78952-124-5
Kate Bush – Bill Thomas 978-1-78952-097-2
Camel – Hamish Kuzminski 978-1-78952-040-8
Caravan – Andy Boot 978-1-78952-127-6
Cardiacs – Eric Benac 978-1-78952-131-3
Eric Clapton Solo – Andrew Wild 978-1-78952-141-2
The Clash – Nick Assirati 978-1-78952-077-4
Crosby, Stills and Nash – Andrew Wild 978-1-78952-039-2
The Damned – Morgan Brown 978-1-78952-136-8
Deep Purple and Rainbow 1968-79 – Steve Pilkington 978-1-78952-002-6
Dire Straits – Andrew Wild 978-1-78952-044-6
The Doors – Tony Thompson 978-1-78952-137-5
Dream Theater – Jordan Blum 978-1-78952-050-7
Elvis Costello and The Attractions – Georg Purvis 978-1-78952-129-0
Emerson Lake and Palmer – Mike Goode 978-1-78952-000-2
Fairport Convention – Kevan Furbank 978-1-78952-051-4
Peter Gabriel – Graeme Scarfe 978-1-78952-138-2
Genesis – Stuart MacFarlane 978-1-78952-005-7
Gentle Giant – Gary Steel 978-1-78952-058-3
Gong – Kevan Furbank 978-1-78952-082-8
Hawkwind – Duncan Harris 978-1-78952-052-1
Roy Harper – Opher Goodwin 978-1-78952-130-6
Iron Maiden – Steve Pilkington 978-1-78952-061-3
Jefferson Airplane – Richard Butterworth 978-1-78952-143-6
Jethro Tull – Jordan Blum 978-1-78952-016-3
Elton John in the 1970s – Peter Kearns 978-1-78952-034-7
The Incredible String Band – Tim Moon 978-1-78952-107-8
Iron Maiden – Steve Pilkington 978-1-78952-061-3
Judas Priest – John Tucker 978-1-78952-018-7
Kansas – Kevin Cummings 978-1-78952-057-6
Led Zeppelin – Steve Pilkington 978-1-78952-151-1
Level 42 – Matt Philips 978-1-78952-102-3
Aimee Mann – Jez Rowden 978-1-78952-036-1
Joni Mitchell – Peter Kearns 978-1-78952-081-1
The Moody Blues – Geoffrey Feakes 978-1-78952-042-2
Mike Oldfield – Ryan Yard 978-1-78952-060-6
Tom Petty – Richard James 978-1-78952-128-3
Porcupine Tree – Nick Holmes 978-1-78952-144-3
Queen – Andrew Wild 978-1-78952-003-3
Radiohead – William Allen 978-1-78952-149-8
Renaissance – David Detmer 978-1-78952-062-0

Also available from Sonicbond ...

The Rolling Stones 1963-80 – Steve Pilkington 978-1-78952-017-0
The Smiths and Morrissey – Tommy Gunnarsson 978-1-78952-140-5
Steely Dan – Jez Rowden 978-1-78952-043-9
Steve Hackett – Geoffrey Feakes 978-1-78952-098-9
Thin Lizzy – Graeme Stroud 978-1-78952-064-4
Toto – Jacob Holm-Lupo 978-1-78952-019-4
U2 – Eoghan Lyng 978-1-78952-078-1
UFO – Richard James 978-1-78952-073-6
The Who – Geoffrey Feakes 978-1-78952-076-7
Roy Wood and the Move – James R Turner 978-1-78952-008-8
Van Der Graaf Generator – Dan Coffey 978-1-78952-031-6
Yes – Stephen Lambe 978-1-78952-001-9
Frank Zappa 1966 to 1979 – Eric Benac 978-1-78952-033-0
10CC – Peter Kearns 978-1-78952-054-5

Decades Series
The Bee Gees in the 1960s – Andrew Mon Hughes et al 978-1-78952-148-1
Alice Cooper in the 1970s – Chris Sutton 978-1-78952-104-7
Curved Air in the 1970s – Laura Shenton 978-1-78952-069-9
Fleetwood Mac in the 1970s – Andrew Wild 978-1-78952-105-4
Focus in the 1970s – Stephen Lambe 978-1-78952-079-8
Genesis in the 1970s – Bill Thomas 978178952-146-7
Marillion in the 1980s – Nathaniel Webb 978-1-78952-065-1
Pink Floyd In The 1970s – Georg Purvis 978-1-78952-072-9
The Sweet in the 1970s – Darren Johnson 978-1-78952-139-9
Uriah Heep in the 1970s – Steve Pilkington 978-1-78952-103-0
Yes in the 1980s – Stephen Lambe with David Watkinson 978-1-78952-125-2

On Screen series
Carry On… – Stephen Lambe 978-1-78952-004-0
David Cronenberg – Patrick Chapman 978-1-78952-071-2
Doctor Who: The David Tennant Years – Jamie Hailstone 978-1-78952-066-8
Monty Python – Steve Pilkington 978-1-78952-047-7
Seinfeld Seasons 1 to 5 – Stephen Lambe 978-1-78952-012-5

Other Books
Babysitting A Band On The Rocks – G.D. Praetorius 978-1-78952-106-1
Derek Taylor: For Your Radioactive Children – Andrew Darlington 978-1-78952-038-5
Iggy and The Stooges On Stage 1967-1974 – Per Nilsen 978-1-78952-101-6
Jon Anderson and the Warriors – the road to Yes – David Watkinson 978-1-78952-059-0
Nu Metal: A Definitive Guide – Matt Karpe 978-1-78952-063-7
Tommy Bolin: In and Out of Deep Purple – Laura Shenton 978-1-78952-070-5
Maximum Darkness – Deke Leonard 978-1-78952-048-4
Maybe I Should've Stayed In Bed – Deke Leonard 978-1-78952-053-8
Psychedelic Rock in 1967 – Kevan Furbank 978-1-78952-155-9
The Twang Dynasty – Deke Leonard 978-1-78952-049-1

and many more to come!

Would you like to write for Sonicbond Publishing?

We are mainly a music publisher, but we also occasionally publish in other genres including film and television. At Sonicbond Publishing we are always on the look-out for authors, particularly for our two main series, On Track and Decades.

Mixing fact with in depth analysis, the On Track series examines the entire recorded work of a particular musical artist or group. All genres are considered from easy listening and jazz to 60s soul to 90s pop, via rock and metal.

The Decades series singles out a particular decade in an artist or group's history and focuses on that decade in more detail than may be allowed in the On Track series.

While professional writing experience would, of course, be an advantage, the most important qualification is to have real enthusiasm and knowledge of your subject. First-time authors are welcomed, but the ability to write well in English is essential.

Sonicbond Publishing has distribution throughout Europe and North America, and all our books are also published in E-book form. Authors will be paid a royalty based on sales of their book. Further details about our books are available from www.sonicbondpublishing.com. To contact us, complete the contact form there or email info@sonicbondpublishing.co.uk